Peter Payne

martial arts

The spiritual dimension

with 108 illustrations, 13 in color

Thames and Hudson

To Kate, with love

I would like to acknowledge with great
gratitude my debt to all those teachers
who have contributed to my study of
the martial arts: William Haugwort,
Kenn Chase, George Mattson, Kazuo
Chiba, Minoru Kanetsuka, John Kells,
Professor Chi, Master Chu, Rose Li, Doug
Lee, and especially my first teacher,
Professor J. G. Vallée of Geneva, who
initiated me into Judo.

I also want to thank all those who
have contributed to my awareness of
the spiritual dimensions of life, in
particular Dhiravamsa, Pir Vilayat Khan,
Sogyal Rinpoche and Namkhai Norbu
Rinpoche.

Special gratitude is due to my
Alexander teacher, Walter Carrington,
for his help and wisdom.

Published in the United States in 1987 by
Thames and Hudson Inc., 500 Fifth Avenue,
New York, New York 10110

Library of Congress Catalog Card Number 86-51575

Printed and bound in Japan by Dai Nippon

Contents

Introduction

There is an important distinction, often inadequately recognized, between the martial arts and simply fighting. The distinction is not one of competence or technique; the martial arts all have their origin as part of a total system of training, the ultimate aim of which was a radical transformation of the very being of the practitioner. Often these roots have been neglected, underemphasized or totally abandoned; nevertheless their spiritual dimension is the heart of the martial arts.

All cultures have a martial tradition which is often linked in some ways with spiritual endeavour (the Greeks included wrestling in the Olympic games, and the hero conquering the monster, demon or evil king is a major archetype of mythology); nevertheless, it is in the East that these arts have achieved their highest peaks and broadest elaborations. It is thought that the martial arts had their origin in India (although little is known of this early stage) and spread (like Buddhism) into China. Here they found a fertile field; the down-to-earth attitude of Chinese culture and the mystical, nature- and body-oriented Taoist religion encouraged the development of a profusion of combat techniques in close connection with the schools of spiritual training. From here the physical and spiritual aspects of the martial arts spread outward, to Mongolia, Indonesia, Java, the Philippines, Korea, Okinawa, and Japan, where they were integrated with the indigenous martial and religious systems to form new and unique entities.

Since around 1900 the martial arts have begun to filter through to Europe and North America, initially from Japan in the form of Judo, and since World War Two in ever greater profusion as secret traditions have become more accessible (even if often watered down) and as popular interest in Eastern thought and wisdom have increased.

Out of this new migration yet further unique forms may grow; Bruce Lee's Jeet Kune Do was greatly influenced by Western boxing, wrestling and fencing, and manifests a very 20th-century image in its rejection of sterile tradition and insistence on efficiency, economy and practical effectiveness. Such integration has also taken place with contemporary Western psychotherapeutic and educational methods, greatly enriching the range of self-development and self-awareness techniques.

To understand the martial arts properly, it is necessary to take account of the psychological and metaphysical as well as the technical aspects. Above all, it is vital to understand how a physical activity, seemingly closely related to the fields of pure sport such as prize-fighting or wrestling, can come to deal with such matters as psychospiritual transformation and the nature of reality. Such is the substance of this book.

1 Technical aspects

The prime importance of the body

One of the greatest contrasts between Western and traditional Eastern cultures is their different attitudes to the body.

In the West, a fundamental split is posited between mind and body. The traditional Christian dogma regards the body as of little value, to be disciplined and abased in order to free the spirit of its constricting bonds. Sex is seen as an impediment, to be avoided as much as possible – often as a tool of the devil. The modern scientific viewpoint reinforces this split: the mind, rational thought and understanding are seen as the ultimate values; the body is merely a vehicle for the mind; emotions only distort the clarity of logic, and one feels the body only when it is going wrong.

In the East, by contrast, the most widespread traditions assert a fundamental unity. Body and mind, spirit and matter, male and female interact in the dance which is the universe. Sexuality is as much a vehicle of spiritual energy as are prayer and fasting. (Hindu Tantrism actually uses sexual intercourse as a meditative ritual, leading to union with the Divine.) And the purification and radiant health of the body are as important to spiritual attainment as are pure thoughts.

Knowledge in the East is seen as having little value unless it is sensed as well as thought. In fact, logical thought has a fairly small place in the scheme of things, even being considered an obstruction during various kinds of experience. Many basic meditations involve concentrating on simple bodily sensations alone.

These two hugely contrasting attitudes now exist, of course, on a small scale within our own culture and often within the individual himself. It is vital to personal and cultural health that this split be resolved; and clearly the martial arts cannot be approached correctly without at least the beginnings of a healing of this wound in our psyche.

In all myth, all religious doctrine, much philosophy and even at the roots of many scientific ideas, we find the great, fundamental awareness of the dual nature within human consciousness and the universe it observes. This dualism has recently acquired scientific backing in the discovery that the right and left halves of the brain (which control the left and right sides of the body respectively) have, in most people, different functions: the left brain deals with the verbal, conceptual, rational aspects of experience, and the right brain with the non-verbal, artistic and intuitive dimension.

This duality, which I would regard as one of the most important and fundamental truths humanity has ever discovered, is perhaps best summarized as a table:

Belly	Head
Body	Mind
Sensation	Conceptualization
Feminine	Masculine
Mother	Father
Child	Parent
Earth	Sky
Hell	Heaven
Nature	Technology
Down	Up
Roots	Branches
Past	Future
Tradition	Change
Mass	Individual
Death	Life
Earth	Air
Inertia	Effort
Gathering energy	Expending energy
Dark	Light
Warm	Cool
Internal	External
Amorphous	Formed
Inclusive	Exclusive
Supporting	Supported
Containing	Bursting
Right brain	Left brain
Left side of body	Right side of body
Artistic	Scientific
Synthesis	Analysis
Soft	Hard
Hypotony (relaxation)	Hypertony (tension)
Yielding	Resistance
Diffusion	Focus
Spoon	Knife

In our culture, as most of us are beginning to realize, one side of this duality is valued and the other devalued. By putting down the Belly side as weak, incapable, unintelligent, insignificant, hysterical, we have created a dangerous imbalance. Deprived of its natural complement, the 'Head' principle becomes cruel, heartless, violent, exploitative, spiritually arid, rigid, dry, insecure and unstable. This manifests in society as crime, war, repression, suicide, the consumer society and a desperate search for 'fun'; in the individual as tension, neurosis, rigid attitudes and various diseases (in particular heart disease).

The repressed and devalued Belly principle is always trying to surface and restore the balance; being opposed, it also becomes distorted and loses its natural character. It may become resistant and heavy, or uncontrolled and hysterical. It will manifest in society as revolution, dissent, ghettoes, cults and (as it achieves more balance) spiritual revival and consciousness-raising movements, as well as body-, feeling- and spirit-oriented therapies; in the individual as unpleasant sensations and emotions, psychosis, an urge to self-abandonment, a rejection of rational thought, certain illnesses (in particular cancer), as well as the drive to seek a path to greater wholeness. Of course all these phenomena are independent, not to be lumped together except insofar as they arise out of this basic dynamic.

While this struggle is going on it may appear as an 'us against them' issue. Those in authority may see themselves as challenged and threatened by the stirrings from below, and the emissaries of the Belly principle may deny any value to the mind and rational thought. Of course the truth lies on neither side exclusively (although it is easy to sympathize with either point of view). Rather, the truth is with the Centre, which is an integration of the two. Modern neurophysiology has discovered that, although the right and left sides of the brain have specialized functions, nevertheless in all ordinary activities *both* sides of the brain are active. It has also been noted that, with the development of the individual towards fuller functioning (whether through meditation or through psychotherapy) the EEG, or brain wave patterns, become more symmetrical, showing the same patterns on both sides.

This integrated state is not simply a balance or alternation between two separate functions; it is not 'half one, half the other' or 'first one, then the other'. It is rather the emergence of a new dimension, a new kind of energy, a new principle, symbolized by the 'Centre', which is a generating force in itself. Just as I have presented a list defining the qualities associated with the principles which I choose to call the Head and Belly principles, so the qualities of this new principle, the 'Heart' principle, can be presented.

Belly	Heart	Head
Body	Feelings	Mind
Sensation	Love	Conceptualization
Feminine	Human	Masculine
Mother	Eternal Child	Father
Child	Adult	Parent
Earth	Humanity	Sky
Hell	Earth	Heaven
Nature	Eco-technology	Technology
Down	Centre	Up
Roots	Trunk	Branches
Past	Present	Future
Tradition	Evolution	Change
Mass	Group	Individual
Death	Resurrection	Life
Earth	Fire and water	Air
Inertia	Action	Effort
Gathering energy	Rhythm	Expending energy
Dark	} Day/night cycle {	Light
Warm		Cool
Internal	Relationship	External
Amorphous	Forming	Formed
Inclusive	Permeable	Exclusive
Supporting	Organic unity	Supported
Containing	Pulsation	Bursting
Right brain	Whole brain	Left brain
Left side of body	Whole body	Right side of body
Artistic	Spiritual	Scientific
Synthesis	Creativity	Analysis
Soft	Resilient	Hard
Hypotony (relaxation)	Eutony (balanced tension)	Hypertony (tension)
Yielding	Integration	Resistance
Diffusion	{ Perception in context }	Focus
Spoon	Fork	Knife

Many of the pairs of polarities listed under the Head and Belly principles do not have an exact equivalent under the Heart principle; the living, organic entity of the Heart principle includes the two other principles as complementary aspects of itself. For instance, true Life (Heart) exists in rhythm between Life (Head) and Death (Belly), just as the whole day (Heart) exists as a pulsation between day (Head) and night (Belly). It is a sign of our cultural bias that we name the whole by the same name as one of its parts; we even call our species 'man', although it is composed equally of men and women. Thus the 'Head' viewpoint may delude itself into considering itself as the whole viewpoint.

The need is for us to regain contact with this central Heart principle, which can restore balance without falling into the trap of over-reaction, counter-reaction, etc. The whole nature of this Way is beyond the scope of this book; but working with and through the body, as in the martial arts, can be an important step in this direction. Interestingly, the martial arts approach can encourage the relaxation, softness, physical sensitivity and intuition so desperately needed by the Head-oriented person; and they can also help develop the focus, precision, concentration and control needed by the excessively Belly-oriented. One should choose a martial art with this in mind; perhaps the style which appeals most at first may not be of the greatest value in terms of one's overall development. For instance, an aggressive, controlling man may be drawn to a hard, external style which may further foster his imbalance, rather than to a soft, internal style which can help him develop what he is lacking (but which he will find extremely difficult to relate to at first).

Having clarified the importance of the Body as a counterbalance to our excessive Head development, we should now take a closer look at precisely what this word 'body' means. We probably take it for granted that we know; but, as with most things, there are very different ways of viewing it.

First, we may see the body from the outside. This is the Head point of view. The body, even one's own body, is seen as an external object among external objects, having particular characteristics of size, weight, shape, colour and movement. What is inside the body may to some extent be palpated from without, but is better seen by cutting the body open, and consists of muscles, bones, organs and other tissues, including the brain, a mass of grey tissue in the skull weighing about three pounds.

From this point of view we may acknowledge the body as the external manifestation of spirit or consciousness; the facial expressions and bodily postures reflect states of consciousness, and even the shape and size of the different body parts provide clues to the thoughts, feelings and past and present relationships of the person 'within' the body (as Bioenergetics and the Alexander Technique have pointed out). In terms of the martial arts, this viewpoint emphasizes the positioning and speed of the limbs, the accuracy of the technique, the force developed in a movement.

But from another point of view, the body is *felt* directly rather than *seen* from without. The body is this directly sensed 'inner' reality, this complex of shifting sensations and feelings that interacts with our thoughts and with the outside world.

This is still too limited a description; for not only our own bodies but those of others, as well as the 'bodies' of all things, organic and inorganic, can be experienced in this way. People skilled at massage can sense in another's body the tensions and areas calling for release; not by sight or touch but by an 'interior', intuitive feeling which has the same quality as sensing one's own body. It is also possible to sense a tree, a car, a piece of fruit as if from within; by allowing a receptive attitude and not trying to focus on or 'obtain' a sensation, one can feel the answer to the question, 'how would it feel to *be* that object?' (in which case, of course, it is no longer object but subject!).

A Head-oriented person may dismiss this as self-delusion or imagination; but it has been proved by modern neuropsychology that ordinary external perception is actually an image built up within the brain, in response to selected cues from the 'external world' (the number of which is very small in comparison to the flood of stimuli entering our sense organs each second). In other words, our normal 'seeing' is very much like 'imagining' or 'dreaming', and certainly does not give an accurate, photograph-like image of a fixed outside reality which 'is' a certain way (see pp. 45–47).

In terms of the person, this *sensed* reality is the life process, which flows within, around and beyond them to interact with other felt beings and things. It is not really internal as opposed to external, because it is not confined by any impermeable boundaries; it is, rather, a different view on the world from that favoured in our culture, a view which may even be denied all validity by those whose sensitivity has deteriorated to the point where they can no longer perceive in this way and are like a blind person who denies that colour exists because they cannot see it.

In terms of the martial arts, this point of view emphasizes the sensing and liberating of one's internal energy flows, the intuitive sensitivity to one's environment, and the capacity to harmonize with one's 'attacker' to the point where combat is transformed into a dance of moving feelings.

These two points of view on the body, the external and the internal, give rise to one of the basic differences between types of martial art.

Internal-external

This is a most important distinction, somewhat difficult for the Westerner to understand, yet vital for correct appreciation, for learning, and for any acquisition of skill in an Eastern martial art.

The external aspect is the most apparent and familiar; it consists of the positioning and movement of the limbs and body, correct technique, muscular strength, speed and so forth; the sort of skill we are accustomed to associating with a quick, powerful young man.

The internal aspect is more difficult to understand; it is hidden, at least to untrained eyes, and is not spectacular in itself (though it may produce spectacular results). It is concerned with breathing, the correct poise and tone of the core body structures (pelvis, trunk, spine and head), the development of *ki* or internal energy and attitude of mind or awareness. These are the inner, subtle factors, which make the difference between technical competence and genius, between know-how and inspiration, between trick and wisdom. The Chinese have a saying: 'they say the martial arts need strength and speed. But if one man defeats many men, how can it be a question of strength? And if an old man defeats a young man, how can it be a question of speed?' Indeed the martial arts are rife with authentic examples of one old man defeating many skilled strong young men, and of people of all ages performing the most incredible feats.

The internal factors are hard to grasp without personal experience. They involve generating the basic internal energy, which can be accumulated within, and then at will directed outwardly to the task at hand. This is like a battery charged with electricity, which can be used to run a gramophone, a light bulb or a hoover, for example. The appliances are the external aspect, the electricity the internal. The internal needs the external in order to manifest itself; the external needs the internal in order to have vital force.

An important distinction is made between the acquisition of localized external strength and the development of internal power. Through prolonged effort and exercise, any one part of the body may be greatly strengthened; there is no doubt that through weight training, for instance, the arms can be developed, giving a spectacular and powerful punch. But this strength is localized, unintegrated with the rest of the body, and cannot change easily from tension to relaxation.

On the other hand, internal energy is stored centrally and can be directed to wherever it is required. It is flexible and changeable, and it integrates the body into one coordinated unit. It can enhance all functions; if directed to the eyes and ears, it sharpens sight and hearing; to the skin, it increases sensitivity; to the abdomen, it develops courage; and it can enable any part of the body to withstand heavy blows. The monk Chueh Yuan, a master of Shaolin boxing said: 'Without ch'i [*ki*] there is no strength. A quack boxer shoots out his hand ferociously, but there is no true strength in his strike. A real boxer is not so flamboyant, but his touch is as heavy as a mountain.' (Robert Smith, *Secrets of Shaolin Temple Boxing*.)

Internal energy is also the primary factor in maintaining good general health; it keeps the internal organs in good condition and increases the body's resistance to disease. It is also the foundation for good mental and emotional health; strong internal energy bestows a radiant, substantial sense of well-being and good humour. Look at the statues of Hotei, the laughing god with a big belly and a sack on his back: his belly is full of internal energy, his heart full of good humour, his sack full of goodies for the children of the world.

Internal energy is developed in many ways. It cannot be acquired mechanically (as muscular strength can be by lifting weights); it is rather something deep and innate that must be allowed to emerge from the well of our inner nature. Kuo Feng-ch'ih, Master of Pa Kua, says: 'Boxing requires movement; but first, the *Internal* requires stillness; to defeat the enemy requires strength; but first the *Internal* requires softness; fighting requires speed; but first, the *Internal* requires slowness'. (Robert Smith, *Pa Kua*.)

Through softness, slowness and stillness the internal is cultivated, nourished by natural, gentle, deep breathing, by ease and freedom in the body core, and by non-grasping receptive awareness.

It manifests as feeling and sensation moving within and around the body (it is possible to experience sensation outside as well as inside the skin). This feeling can have many qualities, depending on the state of the internal energy and on the openness of one's body to it: common sensations are heat and cold, vibration and flow, fullness and emptiness, roughness and smoothness, heaviness and lightness.

While few martial arts are purely external or internal, there are certain arts that emphasize the internal particularly strongly. The Japanese art of Aikido is one; and the three major Chinese internal arts are T'ai Chi Ch'uan, Pa Kua and Hsing-I. Each places strong explicit emphasis on the accumulation and use of internal power, although the external technique in each case is quite different.

It is more difficult to specify techniques that are primarily external; so much depends on the level of instruction and the quality of the teacher. Western boxing and wrestling are certainly external, and nowadays Judo and Karate are often taught without much internal emphasis. In general, the external Chinese arts are classified as 'Shaolin', divided in turn into Northern Shaolin which stresses kicks and leaps, and Southern Shaolin which stresses use of the arms. But in the hands of a great teacher, even Western boxing can become a vehicle for the internal; and a poor teacher can make even T'ai Chi a matter of mere external form.

Reading this may give you a more or less clear *idea* of the internal; but as long as it remains in the head it is *not* the internal. So here is a simple exercise to give you a taste of what is meant by 'internal energy':

Stand erect and relaxed. Begin to shake your wrist as if shaking water off your fingertips, letting the wrist and fingers be completely limp. Then let the elbow go loose, and shake the whole forearm. Next let go of your shoulder, and shake as if your whole arm were a length of rope that you are trying to shake loose from your body. After one or two minutes shaking, relax, stand easily, close your eyes and notice the difference between your two arms. Move your arm around and notice the difference in the quality of movement and in its relation to the air. Touch something or someone with each arm and notice the difference in sensitivity.

Then shake the other arm to balance yourself out.

The differences you feel are due to an increased flow of internal energy in the shaken arm. The increase will only be temporary; it requires more sophisticated techniques and much practice to enhance energy flow permanently. But this exercise will introduce you to the possibilities of the state of natural internal flow; the state that is our birthright, that babies and animals have naturally, that is within reach of all of us.

At advanced levels of an internal art, techniques are developed which are purely internal, with little or no external power being used. These border on the supernatural; the capacity of Uyeshiba (the founder of Aikido) to throw opponents without touching them, the ability to knock opponents down at a distance, the breaking of bricks using only a small, light hand motion, are examples. Other abilities developed through *ki* training are the 'iron skin', in which any part of the body may be made so tough as to resist a sword blow; the 'death touch', in which a light contact can send a lethal charge of *ki* energy to damage the internal organs in specific ways; and 'repelling energy', in which an attacker is automatically thrown away from the master's body with no conscious attention on the master's part. (A story is told of Yang Lu Ch'an, a great T'ai Chi master of the 17th century, who was fishing by a river when two rival masters attacked him. The rivals were thrown thirty feet into the river, but the Master never stirred from his position on the river bank.)

These abilities, though rare, are still demonstrated by contemporary masters, and there are signs that some Westerners are willing to devote the kind of time and energy required to develop *ki* control to this level.

A still deeper level of mastery can be attained. Strictly speaking, this is no longer internal power (*nei-kung*), but mind power (*hsin-kung*). These techniques involve the direct influence of an opponent's mind by one's own thought (rather than action on the opponent's *ki* by one's own energy). A skill developed in some form by most combat sports is an intuitive anticipation of the opponent's next movement; this may be developed to a seemingly telepathic level. Another important ability in terms of everyday self-defence is the art of not inciting aggression − in other words, through one's own mental attitude creating an atmosphere in which the potential aggressor will not have an aggressive impulse.

A Zen story illustrates this point. A swordsmaster wished to test his three students. He took them to a narrow ravine in which a fierce wild horse lived, and told them to come through one at a time while he positioned himself at the other end of the ravine.

The first student started through, and when the wild horse lunged at him he skilfully blocked and dodged the flailing hooves, and won his way through to where the Master was waiting. Proud of himself, he turned and watched to see if his fellow student would put up as good a fight.

But the next student, seeing the horse from a distance, nimbly climbed up the walls of the ravine, passing far above the horse's head. Though he reared and pawed at the rock in fury, the horse could not reach him; and the second student joined his chastened friend next to the Master. Both turned to watch the performance of the next student – which tactic would he follow? Would he engage the horse in fierce combat, or would he craftily avoid the animal's wrath?

The third student appeared at the mouth of the ravine; calm and unconcerned, he walked through the ravine, and the wild horse whinnied in greeting and paid him no further attention.

On a more esoteric level are forms of telepathic hypnosis – the capacity to put someone to sleep, to give them hallucinations, or to make them not notice you at all. These methods were used by the Ninja, the 'secret agents' of Japanese feudal times, as well as by great masters of Korean Hwarang-do and other systems. That such abilities are not mere fantasy is borne out by recent Russian research into the field, as recounted in Ostrander and Schroeder's book, *Psychic Discoveries Behind the Iron Curtain*.

External aspects: techniques

Among the many combat systems evolved by different cultures, there is a tremendous variety in techniques used, in their theoretical bases, in style and in the purpose the system is designed to serve. An exhaustive description would be an encyclopaedic task; even a complete listing would run to many pages. But there are broad similarities between arts evolved in different cultures and also a number of basic categories, which make a general survey possible. The categories largely fall into pairs; those I shall use here are grappling vs. hitting, hard vs. soft, empty hand vs. weapons, the 'Five Animals', and a few miscellaneous, hard-to-categorize arts.

It should be borne in mind that these are arbitrary divisions; rarely will a system be exclusively in one category and not include some of its opposite as well. Even Western boxing has a rudimentary form of grappling (the 'clinch') which can play a key role (as in Ali's wearing down tactics in his 'Thriller in Manila' fight). And many systems are broad enough to include, at advanced levels, many others; for instance, a 1st degree black belt in the modern Juko-ryu Jiu-jitsu must, to pass into the next grade, master an entire new martial art.

Grappling vs. Hitting

Grappling systems include gripping, throwing, ground wrestling and hold-downs, as well as joint-locks, chokes and strangles. Judo is a good example of an art that uses only grappling (at least up to black belt level); Jiu-jitsu, forms of wrestling, Sambo, Chin-na, all emphasize this aspect primarily.

'Pushing Hands' (T'ai Chi)

'Sticky Hands' (Wing Chun)

Lowering one's centre of gravity

Upsetting the opponent's balance (backwards)

Hitting systems include a variety of punching, striking and kicking techniques; blocks, parries and deflections; and evasive bobbing, weaving and ducking. Examples include boxing, Thai kick-boxing, Karate, White Crane, Hsing-I and Atemi.

Almost all techniques employed in the martial arts are covered above, with a few exceptions, discussed on pp. 21–23. A great many systems, especially those that prize practical combat efficiency, will use a combination of both: for instance, stunning with a blow in preparation for a decisive throw or joint-lock. And some systems employ techniques, such as those developed in T'ai Chi's *tui shou* ('Pushing Hands') or in Wing Chun's 'Sticky Hands', which are such a perfect blend of the two that one cannot say if the fighter is striking or throwing, blocking or gripping.

Grappling

I shall begin by discussing grappling, and the various techniques employed within this category.

Gripping   Grappling is necessarily a short-range technique; unlike striking, which can be initiated at distances of up to 6 ft (1.8 m), grappling involves quite close physical contact. Thus in systems that employ primarily grappling there is usually a formalized gripping position, bringing the two combatants into contact with each other, such as the Judo posture (each gripping the opponent's sleeve with one hand and the lapel with the other); the Graeco-Roman upright wrestling position (crouched, one hand cupped on the back of your partner's neck, the other holding his elbow); or the formalized attack positions in Aikido (the attacker gripping the defender's wrist, elbow, neck, for example, in certain defined ways, preparatory to being thrown by the defender). Such positions are partly equivalent to the *kamae*, or readiness postures, used in the hitting arts.

This gripping also serves to control the opponent's movements; naturally if one is using grappling to defend against a hitting attack, it is important not to leave one's opponent freely moving around, able to hit at will. In Aikido, the simple gesture of grasping another's wrist (in early stages used merely as a formalized attack against which the Aikido throw is the defence), is developed into a powerful technique capable of completely controlling the other's offensive ability. Instead of a rigid, hard grasp, the practitioner is taught to grip with a soft, alive hand, as a baby does, almost merging his skin with the opponent's wrist; to use primarily the little and ring fingers, with the index free; then to relax the shoulder and arm and to concentrate all his power at the centre of gravity in the lower belly.

Another aspect of gripping is the use of thumb and fingers to pinch or press certain vulnerable, or vital, points (so-called 'nerve centres' or pressure points – see p. 21). This verges on striking; it may be hard to distinguish a quick thumb- or finger-blow to a vital point from a rapid and powerful pinch. The main difference is that a pinch does not require the prior build-up of momentum in the body to supply power to the attacking hand; thus the pinch may be used in situations where a strike is impractical (for example, at very close range, on the ground or in awkward positions). Often illegal in the more sportive martial art forms, the pinch is an extremely powerful weapon in real-life close combat.

Throwing   Perhaps the most important, and certainly the most spectacular, aspect of grappling, throwing can be seen as a method of using the ground itself to strike your opponent. It is a technique which in many ways favours the smaller,

Turning when pushed (Aikido)

Entering when pulled (Aikido)

Guiding the attacker in a
centripetal spiral (Aikido)

lighter person, since their centre of gravity is below that of their opponent's, and the opponent's balance can thus be disturbed more easily. Moreover, a heavier person will receive more damage from a fall.

The supreme factor in throwing is that of balance. All throwing must begin with upsetting the opponent's balance, which may be done in various ways. (Disturbing psychological balance is very important and may be done in many ways, but since this is crucial to all martial arts techniques it will be discussed later; see pp. 27–29.) The upsetting of physical balance is the specific preparation for a throw (called *tsukuri* in Judo), and any one of eight directions may be adopted: forward, backward, left, right, left front corner, right front corner, left back corner, right back corner. Another important factor is the analysis of the opponent's base of support; his strong direction is along a line joining his two feet, and his weak direction is at right angles to this line.

To upset the balance, a direct application of force may be used to push or pull; in a Sumo match, two mountainous men may crash together with incredible violence in an attempt to knock each other out of the ring. But this is not really good Sumo; in almost all martial arts, skill and subtlety are used rather than direct force.

The basic technique for destroying balance is to use the opponent's own momentum; rather than resisting it, as he expects, you go with it and even help him along. This principle is used to good effect in slapstick movies: Charlie Chaplin in particular is a master. His antagonist has strained in vain to open a locked door – as he draws back to gather momentum for a final shove, Charlie unlocks the door.

In Judo this principle is stated as 'Pull when pushed; push when pulled'. In Aikido the emphasis is on *turning* when pushed (like a door pivoting on its hinges) and *entering* when pulled (moving in on top of the opponent without engaging his force directly).

If the opponent does not have an attacking momentum, but is, for instance, standing still and holding you, a slight variation on the above is necessary; you must create a momentum that you can take advantage of by pushing or pulling against your opponent. When he resists your movement you reverse your direction of force and take him off balance.

A blow, especially to the head, or even a feint, will create unbalance which may be followed up by a throw; the more realistic grappling systems inevitably incorporate such a manoeuvre.

Once the initial unbalance is established, it may be followed up in various ways to complete the throw. The purest and most difficult way is to intensify the imbalance, by gently guiding the opponent's motion, to such a degree that he falls. This reaches its peak in Aikido, where at advanced levels the attacker may be thrown with no physical contact at all. More commonly, the defender lightly holds the attacker's hand or arm, and guides him in a centrifugal or centripetal spiral until he is totally unbalanced and swept off his feet. The defender will often be using a twisting action at the joints similar to joint-locking techniques; but the important difference is that little force is being used and little pain is inflicted; it is not direct power or the threat of damage, but skilful leading that accomplishes the throw.

A simpler way of throwing is to prevent the opponent's initial automatic balance-regaining movements. For instance, in Judo, the following sequence might occur: your partner pushes you; instead of resisting, you unexpectedly step back; off-balance, your partner automatically steps forward to regain his equilibrium; just as his foot is about to touch the ground you sweep it out from under him with the sole

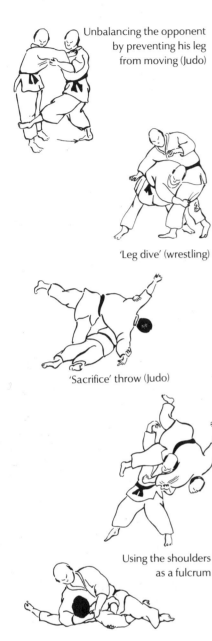

Unbalancing the opponent by preventing his leg from moving (Judo)

'Leg dive' (wrestling)

'Sacrifice' throw (Judo)

Using the shoulders as a fulcrum

Pin using a strong, immobilizing grip

Hold-down, one arm restrained by a joint-lock (Aikido)

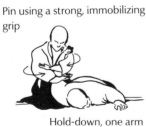

Circular body shift (wrestling)

of your foot. In this type of technique the limb may actually be swept, kicked or hooked away, or simply restrained from moving; in either case, prevented from regaining balance, the attacker falls. The technique may be directed against any part of one or both legs, from foot to thigh; and may use almost any part of your own body. In many Judo throws, it is your own leg or foot that intercepts the opponent's; in the wrestling 'leg dive' or tackle (illegal in Judo because of its tremendous effectiveness), you grip your opponent's knee(s) or ankle(s) with your hands as your shoulder drives him off-balance; and in the Judo 'sacrifice' throws, you throw your whole body on the floor in front of his feet to block his forward movement.

A third way of throwing, closely related to the previous method, is that of the fulcrum. You establish a firm, stable position of your hips, back or shoulders below your opponent's centre of gravity and, using this as a fulcrum, you pivot him or her over into a throw. This is similar to the previous category in that the fulcrum may also prevent balance-regaining movements.

Three other minor points: a joint-lock may often be used to throw with; direct painful pressure on a vital point can force an opponent to the ground; and, as in T'ai Chi, an elastic push can be used to throw someone to the ground, this being half-way between push and throw.

Any of the above methods can employ a weapon, usually a stick, to provide added leverage in the throw.

Ground-work and hold-downs These techniques follow on naturally from a throw. One may wish to restrain a thrown opponent; or if both combatants fall to the ground, the combat can be pursued here. (In any real combat the latter is a strong possibility; many real-life fights consist of untidy rolling around on the floor rather than a clear-cut Western-style exchange of punches.)

The hold-down is designed to immobilize an opponent after a throw, but the form of such techniques varies with the rules of the particular system being used. Many Judo or wrestling pins would not be viable in real combat conditions, where biting, pinching, clawing and gouging are not prohibited. Some pins rely on a strong, immobilizing grip; others on some form of joint-lock, and still others on a flexible, skilful manipulation of one's body weight to control the opponent's movements. Several Aikido throws lead directly into a hold-down, usually with the opponent on his face with one arm restrained by a joint-lock.

Ground wrestling in general is highly developed in Judo and in wrestling. Judo uses many joint-locks and body-weight control techniques, developing a capacity to shift smoothly from one hold to another if the first proves ineffective. In wrestling, many effective techniques used elsewhere are illegal, and a great variety of highly skilful, circular body shifts has been developed. In any formalized ground wrestling, biting, scratching, gouging, kneeing and butting are illegal; naturally in a combat-oriented method they must be included and learned, though realistic practice is very difficult.

Joint-locks Surpassing even throwing in variety and versatility, joint techniques are used in every grappling system. The Chinese Chin-na and Japanese Jiu-jitsu schools especially emphasize locks. They are in general, however, difficult to apply against a stronger adversary; considerable skill is needed before they become practicable in true self-defence, as any lapse from precise positioning and timing

Cranking the arm

Flexing the elbow joint

Leg-lock

Strangle

will render the technique ineffective. The temptation to try to force a failed attempt is great; if you do not immediately flow into a different approach, you are liable to find yourself in a strength-and-weight contest. In combat-oriented systems, an initial stunning blow will often be used as a set-up for the lock.

In a joint-lock, one or more joints of the body are placed in a potentially damaging, stressed position. This gives great control over the opponent's motion: the lock itself drastically limits his or her freedom of action, while the threat of severe pain or damage acts as a further constraint. Thus a lock can be used as a restraint or 'come-along' hold, a throw, a hold-down, or as an incapacitating attack by breaking or dislocating the joint.

There are techniques for locking every joint in the body (except perhaps the jaw and the coccyx!). An exhaustive listing would be prohibitively long, but certain principles can be noted. Perhaps the most common lock is applied by hyperextending the opponent's arm, which stresses the hinge joint of the elbow. The wrist joint can be stressed in five different ways, the outward twist being the most common. The shoulder is also often the target, either using the leverage of the straight arm or by bending the arm at right angles and cranking it. The elbow may also be 'nutcrackered' by placing your forearm inside the opponent's elbow joint and forcibly flexing it. The fingers and thumb may also be bent or twisted.

Similar, though more limited, techniques apply to the corresponding joints of the leg, and the neck can be locked in four different ways; even the back can be locked (as in the 'Boston Crab' of professional wrestling).

Strangle and choke   These are important supplementary techniques, unique in that they can easily produce controlled unconsciousness with little or no risk (if correctly applied by someone with knowledge of Kuatsu, the Japanese revival system). They are an integral part of Judo ground-work, where they reach a high degree of technical sophistication, although they are illegal in wrestling. The ancient sect of Indian assassins, the Thugs (from which we get our word) specialized in Thuggee (strangle and choke), often using a scarf in a combination of throwing, pinning and strangling, which left the victim little chance.

There are actually three different techniques included in this category. The choke is applied by pressure on the windpipe, cutting off the supply of air. It is unpleasant to experience, rather dangerous (as the cartilage of the windpipe could be crushed), and produces unconsciousness within about sixty seconds, from which recovery is spontaneous if the hold is not continued past the point of loss of consciousness.

The arterial strangle applies pressure to the carotid arteries on either side of the neck, which carry blood to the brain. If both arteries are compressed, unconsciousness will ensue in five seconds; again, if not prolonged, recovery of consciousness is usually (but not always) spontaneous. When correctly applied there is no discomfort (indeed, many find it a pleasant and relaxing experience).

In the nerve strangle, pressure is applied to one or both sides of the neck, precisely on a certain nerve ganglion. This induces, via the vagus nerve, a reflex stoppage of the heart and massive loss of blood pressure; unconsciousness is instantaneous. Recovery from this may *not* occur spontaneously; since the heart nerves have received a huge inhibitory stimulus, they may need to be artificially stimulated in order to re-start. In Kuatsu, this may be done by elastic, 45° upwards blows with the heel of the hand in the region of the sixth thoracic vertebra (at the bottom of the shoulder blades).

The upper arm as a natural weapon

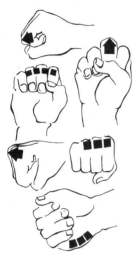

Parts of the hand as natural weapons

'Karate chop' (*shuto*)

Hitting

This is the other major division of martial arts techniques. Compared to grappling, it is a long-range technique, with a certain advantage going to the taller, longer-reaching person. There exists a tremendous variety of techniques and systems within this category. They all use hitting as the primary offensive weapon; this may be done with hands (punching and striking) or feet (kicking).

The essence of hitting is to generate momentum in the body and then to transmit this via a limb and an impact area to the opponent's body. This momentum involves both weight and speed; the physical energy of a blow depends on both the weight of the attacking object and the speed it is moving at, and the speed is more important than the weight. Double the weight and you double the energy of the blow; but double the speed and the energy is multiplied by four.

Many of the more esoteric aspects of the martial arts revolve around this generation of central momentum; many factors are involved, physical and mental, and the energies generated verge on the supernatural. Modern masters can easily deliver a knock-out punch, starting, amazingly enough, with their arm extended straight out and their fist already touching their opponent. They can kill a full-grown bull with one blow, smash a stack of twelve bricks, and swipe the top off a free-standing empty beer bottle.

The most frequently used method of generating momentum is a rapid twist of the hips, entraining the trunk and shoulders and thus firing off the fist like a stone from a sling. This technique often involves rapid extension of the back leg, shooting the whole body forwards as the pelvis rotates. Boxing and Karate favour this approach (though they apply it in different ways).

The other major method is much less well known and very hard to describe. The hips do not rotate, nor does the leg extend strongly, but a kind of springy connection is built up through the whole body. This springiness impels the hand forwards like a quarrel from a crossbow; at the instant of contact the body jerks back away from the hand as the hand shoots forwards, creating an explosive effect like a bullet from a gun. This method is used in Wing Chun and in Hsing-I.

The arm and shoulder muscles are only secondarily involved in many punching methods; the biggest obstacle to developing a powerful punch is the tendency to contract the arm muscles and *try* to hit hard. This slows down the punch considerably.

There are three levels of speed in punching. The first level is the untrained 'wind up and throw it' approach, where the concentration is on the hefty preparation of a haymaker, or swinging blow. It can be seen coming before it has even started towards you, and the trained exponent can counter-strike or block before the punch has built up any momentum.

The second level is, broadly speaking, that of the trained boxer or *karateka* (practitioner of Karate), who unleashes the punch with no give-away preparation and with maximum focus of power into the attacking motion. Here the mental focus is on the attack, not the preparation; a skilled defender will see or sense the punch coming and can block or dodge it, or even counter-punch if he or she is very fast.

The third level is the whiplash. Here the mental concentration of the attacker is not on the preparation, nor on the powerful delivery. Instead, the focus is on the *withdrawal*. The punch must be retracted from the point of impact as fast as possible, and no thought or attention is given to the delivery. The movement of the hand from ready position out to the target is assumed to take no time at all. When correctly executed, this whiplash punch concentrates a penetrating, shocking force into the target; and the defender does not sense it coming, but only sees it (if at all) as it withdraws. Only a quasi-telepathic sensitivity can defend against such a punch. A Chinese martial arts text says: '. . . correct hitting is invisible. The enemy should fall without seeing your hands'.

This punch should be practised with great caution, building speed very slowly, and the arm should *never* be allowed to lock in full extension at the elbow, as the joint could easily be broken or otherwise injured. This punch will extinguish a candle by sucking the flame after it as it withdraws, or will cause a freely suspended piece of paper to sway *towards* you.

Hitting uses a large variety of natural weapons to transmit the impact. Some of these, such as the fingers or the fist, require much training before they can be used properly; others, such as the palm-heel and the elbow, are tough enough to need none. Training the natural weapons is largely a question of acquiring precise alignment and coordination (so that the wrist, for example, is in a straight line and will not buckle on impact), with strength of muscles and ligaments a secondary factor. The development of callouses and toughened skin is largely irrelevant and can be damaging to proper functioning of the hand.

Natural weapons of the arm include the fingertips, the ends of the second knuckles of the index and middle fingers, the knuckles, the little-finger edge of the fist or palm, the thumb, the heel of the hand, the forearm, the elbow and the shoulder. They are used in two main ways: punching, in which the forearm is directly in line with the direction of impact; and striking, in which the forearm is at right angles to the direction of impact (as in the 'Karate chop'). Each of these categories can in turn be divided: punching includes linear punches, in which the hand travels directly to the target along a straight line; and circular punches, in which the hand takes a circular path to the target (as in a hook or a swing). Striking can be divided into forehand and backhand strikes. Punches in general allow a heavier impact, but do not build up as much speed as strikes.

Kicking   In some systems, kicks are used in preference to punches and strikes. The legs are usually slower and less versatile, and kicking leaves you temporarily in a position of precarious balance; however, the legs have a longer reach and are more powerful than the arms. The strongest and furthest-reaching blow in the martial arts is probably the side thrust-kick, and in a slightly modified form it can be very fast as well. In an all-round martial art, kicking and punching will complement each other, the kick usually drawing the opponent's guard low, and the punches, high.

Although kicks do not come in quite the variety that punches do, there are nevertheless many different kinds, basically divisible into thrust-kicks, in which the attacking surface is extended in a straight line towards the opponent; snap-kicks, which use a snapping motion of the knee to strike along a curved path; and round-kicks, in which the entire leg is swung from the hip in a broad circular motion.

Kicks may be delivered forwards, sidewards and backwards, and may be aimed anywhere from the instep to the head (although high kicks are usually eschewed in practical combat because of the danger of loss of balance). There are also some spectacular flying kicks, in which one or both legs kick out as one leaps through the air. Perhaps the most difficult kick is the flying reverse round-house kick (used in, for

Front kick

Side thrust-kick

Flying kick

The head as a natural weapon

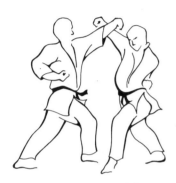

The block used forcefully
(Shotokan Karate)

Block leading into a
counter-attack

instance, Shorinji Kenpo), which combines, simultaneously, jumping, spinning around backwards, and scything the air with the heel of the extended leg. In Bruce Lee's films there are some magnificent high and flying kicks, but he would rarely use such a kick in actual combat.

Natural weapons of the leg include the heel, the edge of the foot, the ball of the foot, the toes, the instep and the knee; even the hip may be used to deliver an extremely powerful short-range blow.

The head should not be left out of this list; solid portions of the skull can be used to great effect in close-range fighting. The head can strike forwards, backwards or to the side in a very unexpected fashion.

In Pa Kua, they have a saying: 'Everything is fist', which perhaps conveys the sense of these descriptions; once the basic central use of the torso is developed, the power of the punch can be channelled out through almost any part of the body.

Blocking   The natural complement to the hitting attack is defensive blocking, in which the attacking limb is diverted from its target by the defender's arm or leg. Blocks vary as much as punches. Some blocks are quite aggressive; in Japanese Shotokan Karate the block may slam against the attacker's arm with sufficient force to break it. A more economical (if less drastic) defence is the parry, in which a light slap diverts the attacking movement so that it misses its target. And the subtlest form of blocking, the deflection, employs a soft, gentle glide to subtly redirect the incoming force.

A block may be used as a purely defensive manoeuvre; more often it will lead into a counter-attack. This may be a throw or joint-lock; the deflection in particular may be used to join one's own movement with that of the attacker so that his momentum is redirected in an unbalanced direction and thence to a throw. But in the context of hitting systems, the counter-attack will be a punch, strike or kick.

The combinations are almost infinite; however, three major categories emerge. First, the opponent's attack may be blocked, then in the next movement, hopefully before he can punch again or withdraw to a defensive position, the defender launches his own counter-attack (usually with the leg or arm that did not block). For instance, he may block with the right hand and then counter-attack with a right front kick.

In the second method, the defender counter-attacks *at the same time* as he blocks. He uses a limb not involved in blocking; for example, he blocks with the left hand and simultaneously punches with the right. This is obviously intrinsically faster than the previous method, although much more difficult to perform.

The last method is much the most difficult; the attack and block become one; the opponent's attack is deflected by the counter-attacking arm. This requires very precise timing and body positioning, but when perfected is an almost unstoppable technique. Many systems use the last two methods at advanced levels, but Wing Chun and Hsing-I in particular place a major emphasis on them.

The legs can also be used for blocking, mostly against kicks; it is hard to block kicks with the arms both because kicks are so powerful, and because they are usually directed lower than the hands can easily reach. When possible, a leg is blocked with a leg.

Evasion   Even more subtle than deflection, evasion is little stressed in most hitting techniques. Western boxing uses it a lot; Aikido in its sword and stick techniques

Simultaneous block and counter-attack

Ducking

The *kiai*

develops evasion to a peak of skill. Evasion involves ducking, bobbing and weaving to avoid strikes and punches; fading or withdrawing to get out of reach of punches or kicks; and whole-body spinning and turning movements to remove oneself from the opponent's line of attack. Evasion is also an integral part of wrestling-type systems.

Vulnerable points   In all hitting systems, some emphasis at least is placed on where to hit. Boxing has little sophistication here, partly due no doubt to the use of padded gloves; the head, the jaw, the heart and the solar plexus are the main targets. Most Chinese and Japanese systems have elaborate and carefully guarded charts of vital points, usually connected with the acupuncture points. Certain systems, such as the 'Drunken Man' system, have developed an incredible sophistication in this field; the points are located very precisely, and the exact place to be attacked depends on the season, the time of day and a snap diagnosis of the opponent's state of health based on various subtle cues. Such an attack might involve only a light touch, but could produce all kinds of precise effects including illness and the 'death touch' (see pp. 22–23). These arts are largely dying out now, but still survive in small pockets here and there.

Again, I would like to stress that it is rare to find a system that uses only hitting or only grappling. In most methods, the two complement each other. It is interesting, however, to consider Western boxing and wrestling; a contest was staged in the 1950s at the University of Illinois between the boxing team and wrestlers in eight weight classes. A bout was regarded as won if the boxer achieved a solid blow to a vital area, or if the wrestler achieved a near fall. Of the eight bouts, seven were won by the wrestlers; the one boxer to win had also been a wrestler. As soon as the wrestler got inside the reach of the boxer's arms, the contest was effectively over. Of course the situation might have been different had the boxers been kickers as well.

Other techniques

There are a few unusual techniques which do not fit into the preceding categories. I would like to say a few words about them.

One important art, which forms a part of many systems but is rarely perfected on its own, is that of Kiai jitsu ('The Technique of the Shout'). *Kiai* is the name given in Japan to the yell that is often used in combat. *Ki* is the internal energy already mentioned, and *ai* means union or integration. (The word 'Aikido' is also composed of these two words plus *do,* or Way.) Thus the *kiai* is a total unification of energy, a full, instantaneous focus of all the faculties of one's being into one act. The Samurai say, 'One stroke, one life'.

Each act, to be a true act, should have one's entire being focussed in it. This is the spirit of the *kiai*, which is the expression in sound of this unification. The shout is generated from the lower abdomen, the *hara*, which is the seat of the vital power. It emerges spontaneously and without obstruction from the depths of one's being and is directed by clear intention to merge with the target. Indeed in the *kiai*, the shouter, shout and target become one; it is not a case of a man trying to shout very loudly, so as to influence someone a distance away. Rather, in that transcendent moment of total intensity, space itself collapses and only the *kiai* exists. (In his fascinating book, *Secret Fighting Arts of the World*, John Gilbey describes his meeting with a master of Kiai-jitsu, a man who could stop a nosebleed with a specific sound. The Master demonstrated his technique on Gilbey, who did not even hear the shout that knocked him out, but came to in a confused state, not realizing at first that the demonstration was already over.)

The *kiai* can be used for many purposes; the intention can use the focussed energy to heal or to hurt. In some Judo *dojos* (schools) the use of the *kiai* to revive an unconscious person is taught along with more orthodox percussive massage (Kuatsu). One is reminded of Christ commanding Lazarus to arise from the dead; the magic and power of the word; the science of mantra; 'In the beginning was the Word'; vibration as the essence of the creative process. One could write a book on the *kiai* alone.

Some authors have attempted to analyse the action of the *kiai* in terms of modern neurophysiology. One can trace neural links which allow the heart and other organ functions to be affected by sound stimulation. I find this very interesting and have no doubt it is part, but only part, of the story. Every new scientific discovery offers new explanations for ancient techniques – and if nothing else is certain, it is clear that the science of twenty years hence will have new, different and probably (I hope) more profound explanations.

According to Musashi (perhaps the greatest Samurai in history), the *kiai* is used before a technique, to gather power and to awe the opponent. Goju-ryu Karate uses a deep, vibrant, growling breath which has similar implications. Bruce Lee's free and creative *kiai*, often resembling birdsong or the screech of a leopard, must be heard to be believed. And Uechi-ryu, an Okinawan Karate school, uses a silent *kiai*, stopping the expulsion of air with a barely audible 'hut' to help focus power into the technique.

Another fascinating system is that of the 'Drunken Man'. In this system, the defender staggers, sways and lurches, giving the impression of a drunkard barely in control of his balance. This has several effects: it disarms the attacker, making him feel he has nothing to fear. It may satisfy his desire for victory; the 'Drunken Man' master may even fall, seemingly under the impact of his assailant's blows (in fact, of course, he will yield in such a way as to receive no hurt). In addition, he offers a very difficult target, which moves in unpredictable and surprising ways, setting up no rhythms and patterns that could be taken advantage of by the attacker.

Often this technique is combined with the 'death touch'. There is a story of an aggressive young man, fancying himself something of a master, who grew incensed when an old man did not scuttle quickly away from his arrogant stride. He abused the old man, and when he did not cringe began to attack him. To the shocked onlookers he seemed to be half killing the old fellow; punches and kicks lashed out, and the old man only succeeded in touching him once, lightly on the foot. Finally, the old man was left in a heap by the roadside as the young blood swaggered on his way. To the onlookers' surprise, as soon as his attacker was out of sight, the old man got quickly to his feet and continued on his way, as sprightly as before.

A few days later the young man fell dangerously ill and in a panic called the doctor. Between them they realized what had happened, and the upshot was (as usual in these stories) that the young man sought out his erstwhile victim, made profuse and humble apologies, was healed, and became the old man's apprentice.

Finally I want to mention the late Bruce Lee and his non-system, Jeet Kune Do ('The Way of the Intercepting Fist'). Lee was indeed a great genius, and his early death was a tragedy. Speculations on the true cause of his death by cerebral haemorrhage are rife, but it seems possible that one factor was his misuse of certain breath-holding *ki* exercises, which should be a warning against unsupervised experimentation.

He had much in common with Musashi; a hot temper, a pugnacious youth, a direct and forthright manner and an emphasis on practical combat as the true test of a technique. From a background of street fighting in Hong Kong, he studied Wing Chun (a highly efficient form of fighting) and other Chinese martial arts, as well as Western boxing and fencing. With single-minded dedication he distilled and simplified, discarding whatever was superfluous and irrelevant ('flowery hands'). He stressed a process of continual change and discovery, emphasizing that everyone should find out for themselves what system works for them, and not accept any other as an ultimate authority. His own Jeet Kune Do, as he himself said, was only a step on the path, and, had he lived another ten years, his art would have changed radically, probably moving towards a greater subtlety and simplicity. With his death, no doubt, some of his fans will crystallize 'Bruce Lee's Jeet Kune Do' into yet another of the rigid forms he inveighed against.

He is an example for all of us, not in his personality or his techniques, but in his insistence on discovering for himself, and his willingness to learn from and yet not be trapped by the classical authorities and masters.

His speed, balance and coordination were extraordinary. He used to demonstrate against Karate black belts; he would stand eight feet away and tell them which hand he would attack with and where. Still he could move in and strike too fast for them to block. Granted, he had not the stature of the old Uyeshiba (the founder of Aikido) or of Cheng Man-Ch'ing (a great T'ai Chi master who died a few years ago), but for a man of his age (he was only 32 when he died) he was unique. He never lost a fight – the few who might have beaten him (such as the two mentioned above) would have no investment in proving themselves and would not have challenged him in the first place.

Hard vs. soft

The division of the martial arts into hard styles and soft styles somewhat overlaps with the external/internal division, in that external styles tend to be hard and internal ones to be soft. But this is by no means universally or necessarily true. What is meant by 'hard' and 'soft' is two different ways of using energy, whether this energy is internal (*ki*) or external ('strength').

In general, these two ways of using energy are, respectively, *linear* and *circular*, though some techniques combine elements of both. Linear energy is direct, piercing, angular, abrupt, like a bullet or a battering-ram; circular energy is tangential, sweeping, continuous, like a tidal wave or a whirlwind.

A typical hard system, such as Karate, will emphasize the capacity to generate great muscular tension and intense concentration ('focus'), as well as a mental/ emotional state of total involvement which may approximate a sort of controlled ferocity. The movements will be very quick and snappy. Much use will be made of powerful, direct blocks which could break an arm; and the punches and kicks will be direct and powerfully penetrating. Any throws or locks used will be direct and abrupt, geared towards creating a violent impact.

In contrast, a typical 'soft' system, such as T'ai Chi, emphasizes complete relaxation and suppleness, an expanded, open awareness which includes rather than concentrates, and a mental/emotional attitude of calm, detachment and harmony. Movements will be flowing and continuous. No direct resistance is offered; the aggressor, finding no place for his attack to land, is swept around and away like a leaf in a storm. Throws and locks will simply merge with the attacker's momentum and guide him spirally to the ground; punches and kicks will be more like pushes which fling the opponent away without any sharp point of impact.

I would add that a soft system, like T'ai Chi or Aikido, can easily convert the push into an extremely hard punch, or the soft landing into a damaging one, whereas the hard style has much more difficulty softening its techniques when necessary. In fact, many systems, such as Goju-ryu Karate, (which means 'Hard-soft School'), and Korea's Hwarang-Do, incorporate both kinds of techniques.

In comparing the efficacy of the different schools, the Chinese say: 'Soft beats hard; hard-soft beats soft; and hard beats hard-soft'. Like any generalization about the martial arts, this is probably not true; and anyway, only individuals compete, systems never. But the statement comes from the very Chinese perception that, as in the 'scissors-paper-stone' game, there is no 'best', but only relative judgments; to any technique, there is always a counter-technique, which can in turn be countered; so best not to cling to any one position, as sooner or later you'll be beaten.

Another aspect of the difference between hard, linear and soft, circular methods is rather more technical; it concerns interior-line and exterior-line approaches. If you are standing facing your opponent, hands held forward in an 'on-guard' position, then the parts of your body accessible to attack can be divided into interior and exterior. The interior includes the centre-line and the whole front of your body; the exterior includes the sides and back of your body. If the opponent extends an arm straight towards you, passing between your arms, he or she is 'inside' you; if he loops a swing around outside your guard, aiming for the side of your head, he is 'outside' you. If you block his attack so that, for instance, his left arm is pushed to his left, opening up his guard, this is an 'interior' block; if you block his left arm across his body towards his right, probably turning him somewhat side-on to you, this is an 'exterior' block. Hard styles tend to use compact, elbows-in stances and interior-line attacks and defences, driving directly in, up the centre-line, to attack vital points; soft styles, on the other hand, tend to use more expanded, rounded stances, to punch and block in a circular, exterior-line fashion, and to initiate throws or locks from this exterior position.

Examples of these techniques in fairly pure form are the T'ai Chi 'Pushing Hands' exercise and Wing Chun's 'Sticky Hands'. In 'Pushing Hands', you each touch the other's right wrist lightly with the back of your own, holding the arms in a gentle curve in front of your body; you circle back and forth, each thus remaining outside the other, and attempt to break the other's balance by pushing and yielding.

In 'Sticky Hands', you face your partner squarely and, keeping both elbows close to your centre-line, you interlock wrists with your partner – right to left and left to right. The exercise becomes a complex game of trying to get inside your partner's guard and attack his centre-line while keeping him outside yours.

Each technique has its advantages and disadvantages, and most systems develop both to some extent.

Empty-hand vs. weapons

An important division in the martial arts is between those that use weapons and those that do not. Many systems do indeed use only the empty hand: for instance, Judo, boxing, Shotokan Karate. Other methods may use weapons only as an occasional or optional training system, as in the use of the staff by Wado-ryu Karate.

This type of system often emphasizes forging the natural weapons of the body into the equivalents of clubs and knives. In Okinawa, Karate evolved during the many periods of occupation by foreign powers. As the people were forbidden weapons, they adopted the doctrine: 'Since they forbid us spears, let every finger become a spear; since they forbid us clubs, let every fist become a club; since they forbid us swords, let every hand become a sword!'

Some systems, especially hard and external styles, stress physical conditioning of the limbs, developing hard lumps of callous on the knuckles and sometimes going so far as to break the middle finger to shorten it, creating a better alignment of the fingertips. This approach, besides being positively damaging to the hand, is unnecessary; through correct alignment, muscle control, breathing and visualization, the unprotected hand can easily break brick and stone.

Some other systems confine themselves to one or more weapons, making no use of empty-hand techniques; for instance, Kyudo and Kendo (Japanese archery and sword-fighting). But more frequently, a single system embraces both approaches; for instance, T'ai Chi, best known for its solo weaponless exercise, also has a sword form, a cutlass form, a spear form and a stick form.

In weapon systems, there is an interesting interplay between the form of the weapon itself and the principles of its use. To some extent the weapon itself dictates how it is to be used. Clearly weapons as diverse as the whip, the bow and the throwing star each require specific technical skills. Even different shapes of sword imply different ways of use; the straight sword in the T'ai Chi sword form is used in piercing, precise, linear movements, while the curved sword of the cutlass or 'knife' form is used in circular, slashing movements inappropriate to the straight blade.

At the same time, identical underlying movement principles may be applied to the use of various weapons. This is the case with the aforementioned T'ai Chi forms; the same basic principles of movement are applied despite the differing external forms. We can see this to an extreme extent in Aikido and in the Filipino art of Kali or Escrima, in which the same movements are applied with equal effect to empty-hand, stick and sword techniques.

On occasion, the characteristic movements of a system may determine the form of the weapon. In Pa Kua, a Chinese internal system which is totally circular, consisting of continual circling, twisting and spiralling motions of the whole body, none of the conventional weapons would fit the movements of this unique art. So a form of sword was especially designed, its shape (two intersecting crescents) adapted to the Pa Kua circling movements.

Perhaps the best-known weapon is the Japanese Samurai sword. Its form evolved hand-in-hand with the secret fighting schools; in its earlier stages it was straight, and it went through many changes in degree of curve. Its classical shape, with its subtle, organic curve, is adapted for both slashing and piercing attacks. The quality of the crafting of the metal blade has never been equalled; the making of a good sword was a peak of spiritual creation.

Different swords have different characters – some malevolent, some benevolent. Holding a good blade one can feel its power, its spirit; such a weapon is a touchstone for one's own development. Only through developing a firm centre within oneself, and merging with the sword from this centre, can one handle the weapon with confidence.

This leads us to the key to all weapons systems: merging oneself with the weapon. The weapon must become an extension of one's own body, as intimate as hand or foot; one's *ki*, or internal energy, must flow into the weapon itself.

In Aikido, a simple exercise can demonstrate the effectiveness of this approach.

Grip a stick by one end, hold it horizontally, and have a partner take the far end and push straight in towards you as you resist their force. Note how it feels to do this. Next, imagine the stick as an extension of your arm – a very long finger perhaps – and let your awareness go right to the tip of the stick. Really try to feel or imagine that you are there, right at the end. Maintaining this feeling, have your partner push towards you again, with the same force as they did before. Notice the difference in the ease with which you can resist. If you like, go back and forth between these two methods to get a clearer sense of the change.

This identification with the weapon gives a much greater sensitivity and control than can be achieved by thinking in terms of holding an inanimate object. With this approach, almost anything that comes to hand may be used as a weapon, a fact that is often stressed in practical self-defence teachings. There are formalized Chinese techniques using an umbrella, a fan, a pipe or a wooden bench for combat. Indeed some present-day weapons were originally ordinary everyday utensils; the *nunchaku*, popularized by Bruce Lee, originated as a flail for threshing wheat (see p. 91). In real-life self-defence, keys, an ashtray, the edge of a book, a pen, even a tightly-rolled newspaper can be effective weapons.

The Five Animals

The Chinese martial arts have always been closely associated with health practices as well as practical combat, and most systems combine the two purposes.

Some systems developed directly from the inspiration of watching an animal; for instance, the Monkey system imitates that animal's agility in leaping and rolling, and its ferocious method of attack, tearing at the throat and groin. The Praying Mantis school copies the poised, hypnotic weaving of its namesake, hooks the fingers into imitations of the mantis' claws, and darts out suddenly with the snappy speed of an insect catching its prey. Even the subtle, yield-and-bounce-back approach of T'ai Chi in combat is supposed to derive from a carefully-observed combat between a bird and a snake: each time the bird's beak darted out, the snake yielded flowingly, coming forward again as the bird drew back, until the bird was so exhausted by its efforts that it was easily overcome.

Around the 5th century AD when Buddhism was brought from India to China, the missionary-monk Bodhidharma stayed at the Shaolin Temple and taught the monks certain martial exercises for health, vitality and spiritual development. The exact form of these exercises is a mystery; many claim to teach the originals, but it is hard to say whether they have survived for 1500 years unchanged. In any case, through the years these movements were combined with and modified by native Chinese systems, and in the 13th century were formulated at the Shaolin Temple into the Five Animals system. This approach took the point of view that man has five basic systems, all of which must be developed and integrated for true health. As a martial art, this approach combined soft and hard, internal and external. The five animals were the dragon, the snake, the tiger, the leopard and the crane.

The Dragon form was for the development of *shen*, often translated as mind, heart or spirit; perhaps 'awareness' would be a suitable word. This form used slow, soft movements, like a magical dragon floating through the air. It may have resembled T'ai Chi, and was the most spiritual of the forms, in some sense the ruler of them all.

The second animal was the Snake. This form developed the *ki*. The movements were sinuous, circular, continuous, like a snake coiling and writhing. Although soft and fluid, the motions had a reserved inner power which would give them an irresistible, supple strength if opposed. It probably resembled Pa Kua.

The third form was that of the Tiger. Here, the bones, the most solid and powerful part of the body, were developed. Movements were both fast and slow, often with extreme dynamic muscular tension. The posture was contained and solid, the attacks ferocious, the overall feeling one of implacable power. It may have resembled Uechi-ryu Karate (see p. 85).

The next form was that of the Leopard. Its quality was strength, an agile muscular power reminiscent of the leopard which, while not having the weight and solidity of the tiger, nonetheless has the capacity to leap suddenly, to attack and withdraw quickly, to use its muscular power to generate rapid and strong movements. Of contemporary arts, it resembled Japanese Karate.

The fifth and last animal was the Crane. The function developed was referred to as 'the sinews'. This I believe included the connective tissue or fascia of the body, which, apart from forming the muscle tendons and the joint ligaments, also holds the whole body and its organs together into an integral network. This system was responsible for correct posture and carriage, and gave rise to an overall feeling of integration or disintegration (it is this system upon which the postural techniques of Rolfing and Postural Integration are based). The movements of the Crane form involved an erect, poised trunk, much balancing on one leg, and rapid precise pecking jabs of the hand as well as wing-like blocks and sweeps. It may have resembled the modern White Crane system.

Strategy and tactics

This is an area of the martial arts that is vitally important in all combat techniques and yet receives relatively little attention. The basic question is, having at your disposal a formidable array of offensive and defensive weapons, when and how do you use them? Distance and timing are the crucial variables. All these considerations are to do with fundamental principles which apply to armies as well as to individuals and are applicable on a variety of levels in many fields apart from the martial.

Distance starts with one's own personal space, one's territory as it were. This may be considered as occupying various regions but the first, most important space is that inside one's skin. Certainly this space must remain inviolate if one is to be free from harm (or at least one must have complete control over who or what enters this space and in what manner). Issues of physical healing or damage, nourishment and poison, intercourse or rape, arise here.

In fact in order to have control over this internal personal space it is necessary to control the space around the body; indeed in most cultures a person's private space includes a variable region around them. In terms of the martial arts, this external personal space is defined by the distance within which an aggressor could strike you directly without having to take a preparatory step forward. This crucial distance is the opponent's arm- or leg-reach plus 3 in. (7.5 cm.). In combat terms, if an opponent enters this field, you must either withdraw, neutralize him or attack.

A larger dimension of your space is the awareness field, which is the whole expanse of which you are currently aware. One should always let the awareness field be as wide as possible; in this way one will not be surprised. No action, physical or mental, is taken against potential aggressors in this space; indeed, if one is not to invite attacks upon oneself, it is very important that a spirit of harmony be maintained. Centredness and firmness are established at the core of one's internal personal space; an elastic, resilient quality pervades one's external personal space; and the awareness space is pervaded by a harmonious openness.

The crucial section of an attack trajectory is that in which impact or contact will cause damage; for instance, at the outset of a punch in, say, the first 12 in. (30 cm.), it will not have built up enough energy to cause any damage. Similarly, after it has passed the intended impact point by about 6 in. (15 cm.), the antagonist will have lost his balance and again the punch will have little damaging force. These limits are known as the inner and outer limits of power. So the crucial problem in attack is to bring your attack trajectory (between the inner and outer limits) into contact with your opponent's body (inner defence perimeter); and the problem in defence is to remove your body from his attack trajectory.

These problems can be solved in a great many ways. Simple direct retreat or advance may serve, but lack subtlety and have various disadvantages. Much depends on timing in advance; wrong timing opens you to a simultaneous counter-attack. In defence, a direct retreat may remove you from the attack and give a chance of escape, but, should you wish to neutralize or counter-attack your opponent, you will have to advance again. A better strategy in defence is the angular withdrawal, in which you step back and to the side, getting out of immediate reach of the attack while remaining in an advantageous position for countering. Still better is the circular response, in which one and the same movement becomes withdrawal and counter – just as when you push on a revolving door it withdraws from your push and in the same motion hits you from behind.

The issue of timing, which deals essentially with the relationship and coordination of your movements with those of your opponent, brings us to the fundamental Eastern concept of 'yin' and 'yang'. This refers to the two complementary characteristics of nature, seen as up and down, back and forth, strong and weak, day and night, in and out, and so on. These are in ceaseless active alternation, as may be seen in any natural, cyclic process. In combat, the attack is yang, the yielding, yin. Obviously, according to the law of complementarity, if your opponent is yang, you take a yin state. The attack is met, not with resistance (which would only increase the impact), but with soft, yin evasion or yielding.

But, again according to natural law, yang follows yin and yin follows yang. In the initial stages of 'winding up' and preparing the punch, the aggressor is yin; he is withdrawing his energies (preparatory to sending them out as a punch). In this phase, the prospective victim should naturally become yang – he can then follow the withdrawing energies in and forestall his opponent's attack. (Naturally, this highly effective tactic requires excellent timing and very clear perceptions.)

Similarly, after the attack (yang) has been launched and met only evasion (yin), the attacker becomes yin; he either loses his balance with the force of his blow, or he withdraws to prepare another attack. Whichever he does, his opponent can take advantage of this yin state to change to yang and counter-attack.

Once this simple principle is grasped, many permutations are evident: one arm can be yin (yielding) and the other simultaneously yang (attacking), or an arm can be yin and a leg yang, or even one limb can be simultaneously yin and yang. And then there are the manifold possibilities of feints and deceptions, which are too complex to describe here.

It is important to realize that, at the deeper levels of the martial arts, the point of all these strategies is to develop an intuitive sense of the universal laws. The deepest aim is not simply to defeat opponents, but to come to the Way ('Do' or 'Tao'), which is 'the way the universe works'. Unlike the traditional 'scientific' viewpoint, the 'way it works' is not a mechanical, rational way which has little value as a guide for living one's daily life and dying one's life's death. The Way is a felt and intuited Way, which cannot accurately be expressed in words. It is an organic and transcendent Way, at the same time universal and profoundly intimate, of supreme practical use in life and in death.

Let me try to make it clearer still; through the simple, sensitive physical practice of the martial arts techniques that embody these principles (T'ai Chi's 'Pushing Hands' is a good example), one comes to experience in one's body and feelings an intuitive sense of flow, complementarity and harmony, which is a kind of knowledge. And this knowledge concerns bodies, relationships and feelings, and is universally applicable to all realms of human action. As Miyamoto Musashi says, 'if you know the Way broadly you will see it in everything'.

2   The martial arts as spiritual and psychological disciplines

Warrior of the spirit

The exigencies of combat place great demands on the capacities of the warrior. These demands can act as powerful learning situations for self-discovery and self-confrontation, and may be used to further the spiritual endeavour.

Perhaps the most important of these is the confrontation with death. We are all confronted with death in each loss or change in our lives, but such confrontations we can easily evade, dealing perhaps with the specific change without coming to grips with the principle of change which implies our personal death.

We shall all be confronted one day with our own deaths in the most direct and powerful way – but this will usually be a sudden, rather irrevocable and inconvenient event, of little use (from the point of view of this lifetime) in a training programme.

All spiritual systems set up a confrontation with death; the basic preparatory practices of Buddhism involve the remembrance that one's life is short and of uncertain duration, that one may die tomorrow. In the Chöd rite of Tibetan

Buddhism, practitioners visit a Tibetan graveyard at night (where the corpses are left exposed to the elements and scavengers) and invite the demons to come and take them.

In the West, death is one of the great taboos; constant violence in films and on television negate the reality of death through constant repetition of stereotyped death scenes, and the media numb our imagination with accounts of deaths on a vast scale and under horrific circumstances. Paradoxically, this numbing of the appreciation of death also numbs the vivid appreciation of life. Those who take to danger sports (such as car-racing, mountaineering and sky-diving) often report recapturing a keen, fresh awareness of life and its beauties as a result of their brushes with death.

In the martial arts, of course, death is a constant presence. The whole activity revolves around it. Attack, defence and counter-attack are all performed as if a true life-or-death situation were involved. With proficiency, the vigour of the actions increases and, if one is using weapons, one may employ, for instance, a 'live' (naked) sword instead of a bamboo or wooden sword; all of which make the situation genuinely dangerous.

The confrontation with death is perhaps the most important element of spirituality.

First, death reveals the ego. That part of us which grasps and holds on, which attempts to crystallize the flow of life and box it into separate entities, is totally panicked by death. Fear is the basis of this holding and contracting, and death, or the thought of death, brings out this fear. In fact the fear we feel at the thought of death is not created by the situation but only brought out of hiding; it was there all along in our life, underlying all the rigidities, the pettinesses and the little neuroses (as well as that great neurosis which makes all of us think of ourselves as beings fundamentally separate from our environment and from other people). That fear, which is the lynch-pin holding the whole rigid structure in place, is revealed in the face of death, and can then be looked into and dealt with.

The fear of death is the greatest of obstacles for the martial artist. This fear has a quality of rigidity, or paralysis, or of the loss of control; one may freeze with terror, or one may panic and react blindly and irrationally. Either reaction, intruding at the crucial moment in combat, will spell death, even for the technically accomplished fighter.

But freedom from this incapacitating fear releases great powers. There is a story of a Master of the Japanese Tea Ceremony from the province of Tasa – a man of no martial skill yet of great meditative and spiritual accomplishment. He accidentally gave offence to a high-ranking Samurai, and was challenged to a duel. He went to the local Zen Master to seek advice. The Zen Master told him frankly that he had little chance of surviving the encounter, but that he could ensure an honourable death by treating the combat as he would the formal ritual of the Tea Ceremony. He should compose his mind, paying no attention to the petty chatterings of thoughts of life and death. He should grasp the sword straight-forwardly, as he would the ladle in the Tea Ceremony; and with the same precision and concentration of mind with which he would pour the boiling water onto the tea, he should step forward, with no thought of the consequence, and strike his opponent down in one blow.

The Tea Master prepared himself accordingly, abandoning all fear of death; when the morning of the duel arrived, the Samurai, encountering the total poise and fearlessness of his opponent, was so shaken that he promptly begged forgiveness and called off the fight.

The outcome of the fight, had it taken place, is by no means clear; technical skill could well have been overshadowed by the freedom and concentration of one who no longer feared death.

In the Buddhist tradition, the preparatory practices of the remembrance of death are regarded as being the great motivators on the path; this is why they are essential. Awareness of the reality and inevitability of one's personal death can be a fantastic energizer, releasing unsuspected levels of motivation for radical change. Don Juan, the Yaqui Indian teacher in Castaneda's books, makes the same point with great clarity and power. Don Juan was trying to tell Castaneda that the remembrance of his death is of the utmost importance for the proper conduct of life, while Castaneda protested that it is meaningless to worry about one's death. Don Juan answered,

'I didn't say that you have to worry about it.'
'What am I supposed to do then?'
'Use it. Focus your attention on the link between you and your death, without remorse or sadness or worrying. Focus your attention on the fact that you don't have time and let your acts flow accordingly. Let each of your acts be your last battle on earth. Only under those conditions will your acts have their rightful power. Otherwise they will be, for as long as you live, the acts of a timid man.'
'Is it so terrible to be a timid man?'
'No. It isn't if you are going to be immortal, but if you are going to die there is no time for timidity, simply because timidity makes you cling to something that exists only in your thoughts. It soothes you while everything is at a lull, but then the awesome, mysterious world will open its mouth for you, as it will open for every one of us, and then you will realize that your sure ways were not sure at all. Being timid prevents us from examining and exploiting our lot as men'.

The realization that one is to die and therefore has limited time can cut away an immense amount of pettiness and self-indulgence from one's life. All those thoughts people have at the time of death, regrets over wasted time and lost opportunities, over risks not taken and inertia given in to, all those 'if only I could do it over again' thoughts, can be brought into the present, before the opportunities are past, while the gates are still open, and can galvanize one to begin taking responsibility for living a fulfilling life.

Death is the great changer, the one who ensures that things will not remain static, stagnant, fixed. In the evolution of life on earth, sexual reproduction makes its appearance at the same time as death. Continual, unchanging self-replication (as in the amoeba, which divides to produce identical copies of itself) is a zombie-like living death of sameness and stagnation; the freshness and newness of each unique individual born, who dies to make way for another unique being, is eternally changing life through death. As Christ says, he who tries to save his life shall lose it. The person who clings to the past form, thought or feeling, loses the ever-new, spring-time quality of the unimpeded current of life.

Creative destruction

Tales of the exploits of great martial artists approach the mythic. It was common practice for a caravan, traversing bandit-infested country, to hire one master to guard them. Such a man was capable of repelling the attacks of fifty or a hundred armed men. Even historically recent masters are said to have attained almost supernatural powers. It is said of Tung Hai-ch'uan, the first known Pa Kua master, that one day he was sitting in a chair, leaning against a wall, when the wall suddenly collapsed. His students rushed up, fearing for his life; but he was found to be sitting calmly in the same chair, leaning against another nearby wall.

Still more recently, the Aikido Master, Uyeshiba, was certainly a man of mythic proportions. There are many stories of his incredible feats, which are scoffed at by sceptics; but there is a strip of film, showing the Master as an old man of about 75, no more than 5 ft (1.52 m.) tall, being charged from both sides, at top speed, by two large Judo black belts. Projected in slow motion, successive frames show the Master standing calmly while his attackers inch their way forward. But, just as they are about to grab him, *between two frames* he has moved several feet out of the way and is facing in the other direction. The two black belts continue their rush, to collide violently into each other, while the Master watches. Such a movement, which from the film testimony must have taken *less than one-eighteenth of a second*, demonstrates a transcendence of the normal laws of time and space, a penetration of this world by the magical world of the eternal, the world of myth and archetype.

An outsider's interpretation of the martial arts is often that one learns to defeat one's opponent. But, as Bruce Lee says, 'punches and kicks are tools to kill the ego'. The true opponent to be overcome is oneself – one's petty ego, fears and frustrations, self-limiting concepts, all that constricts one's consciousness. In Karate training, the aspirant may go through a form of training in which he repeats a formal exercise (or *kata*) to, and far beyond, the point of exhaustion. He reaches a point, if he persists, where he simply no longer has the strength to maintain his tense habits of contracting body and mind, and his movement takes on a naturalness and fluidity he had not suspected possible. His perception clears, no longer hampered by the categories and fixations of his normal consciousness, and the world becomes fresh and new. He can never be the same after such an experience; the boundaries of the possible have been pushed back, and he will never believe in his limitations as rigidly fixed walls. His world, and he himself, have been rendered more permeable.

This is also the heroic task of myth. Myths describe the deep, inner transformations of the person, metamorphoses of the psyche which open the doors of consciousness to the world of archetypes, of inspirations and ideals, a world in some sense prior to our everyday physical reality. Myths are tales of spiritual growth, and catalogue the tests and trials, the monsters to be overcome and the rich treasures to be gained by whoever undertakes this journey. The events are not to be taken as describing (not even as faultily describing) physical reality, but refer to the inner changes which must precede any radical world change. The monsters and giants that the hero overcomes are the monsters of his own fears and negativities, the giants of his own inertia or suppressed power. And through this direct facing and overcoming, he can re-own his lost parts and, becoming whole, gain access to the treasures of his own inherent nature.

This points again to the importance of death as the source of life. We have all disowned and split off parts of ourselves, projecting our power out onto the world or repressing our wisdom deep within our unconscious. These split-off parts can seem like real, separate entities, internal or external, and can seem to oppose and threaten us. The quest for wholeness, as described in myth as well as in Jungian psychology, involves first, the realization that these parts are not truly external but are our own projections; and second, the re-owning and re-integration of the parts. We ourselves, as we take ourselves to be prior to this re-integration, are a part; and to become whole, each part must die as a separate being in order to awake to a new life as part of a much greater whole. Thence comes the necessity for us to 'die before our death'; and equally the necessity for us to slay the dragon/giant/opponent, that we may come to fuller life.

The martial artist must realize that in confronting his opponent he confronts himself. The fears, uncertainties and weaknesses are his own, and are not to be projected onto the opponent. Aggression and arrogance must also be recognised for what they are; martial artists are enjoined never to show off, threaten or intimidate; indeed never to use their skill except in dire necessity. The 'macho' type who sees challenges to his skill all around him, who sees others as arrogant and aggressive and is eager to demonstrate his superiority, has not begun to confront his own fears and maintains a state of internal conflict and separation which totally prevent any real mastery. In all the martial arts there is a great stress on humility. This naturally goes together with the acquisition of great powers of combat; such power in the service of an inflated ego would be disastrous. This is also emphasized in spiritual development; often the acquisition of specific psychic powers is regarded as a positive hindrance, as these powers may increase the ego's sense of self-satisfaction and control.

At a deeper level, humility and 'poverty in spirit' may be positively necessary for the development of certain capacities. Just as a substance needs an appropriate container to receive it, so a process of 'emptying out' must precede a new filling. Robert Smith was advised by his teacher, the great T'ai Chi Master, Cheng Man-Ch'ing, to 'invest in loss'; in the technique of 'Pushing Hands', for example, each in turn tries to unbalance the other while 'yielding' and offering no resistance to his partner's push. An expert in this technique offers no firm surface to be pushed; he feels like water or smoke, and no force can damage him. But acquisition of this skill necessitates investing in loss; to be willing, when pushed, to offer no resistance even if this means being flung violently to the ground. Persisted in, this 'non-doing' will result in an amazingly soft and supple body, and you will no longer be pushed over. But let the slightest resistance to being pushed creep in, the slightest tension, and you will again become vulnerable to the opponent's attack.

Both aspects of the mythic path, the hero's journey, are revealed in the martial arts: the fearless facing and overcoming of the monster, and the willingness to be undone, dismembered, to die before death, in order to gain a fuller life.

Developing the will

The will is the means whereby one channels and focusses one's energies into the world and towards some specific action. It is a much misunderstood and misrepresented topic in Western culture – we have a legacy from the Victorian era of conceiving will as 'will-power', a sort of tense, teeth-gritting effort, which bears no resemblance to the various aspects of true will. The true concept of will is most closely related to the concept of *intention*; to intend something, to choose it, to want it, to be directed towards it, all convey the use of the will. In a way one could say it is a mental thing, but it is not conceptual or intellectual. That is to say, it is not a question of thinking about something or of talking to oneself about it, but rather a commitment of one's *self* towards something. It is not a feeling, though it may entail feelings; and it is not physical, though it may have physical effects.

Both in the martial arts and in spiritual development, the will is seen as very important. Clearly the hero must have a well-developed will, both to overcome the trials and adversities he is faced with, and to be capable of sacrificing himself. The martial arts are based on will; from the capacity to go beyond one's limits to the details of correct execution of an individual technique, all depends on will.

Roberto Assagioli, founder of Psychosynthesis, sees three basic aspects of the will: the skilful will, the good will and the strong will. I will deal with each in turn.

The skilful will

By and large the martial arts do not depend on brute force, but on skill. How to use one's energy efficiently and effectively is also part of the study of meditation. And this skilful approach depends in large part on the skilful will.

There is a fairy story about a princess shut up in a tall, unclimbable tower with no door, and a prince who fell in love with her. How were they to be joined? No direct assault was possible; the walls were impenetrable and as smooth as glass; no ladder could reach so high. So the prince took a silken thread and tied one end of it to a snail, which inched its way up to the waiting princess. She untied the thread and began to pull it up; the prince then tied a length of slender string to the silk thread. When she got hold of the string, he tied a rope to the string, which she again hauled up, and so they made their escape.

The point of this story is that in a skilful way they began with the subtlest, easiest level, which can then easily entrain the next level, and so on; avoiding the frustration and failure of an effort-filled, straining attempt to batter down the walls or to throw a heavy rope to that height. This subtle, delicate level of the intention can be sensitive and flexible, finding out the right angle for a throw or a punch, sensing the weak points in an opponent's defence, exploring the line of least resistance. Here the will is like a soft mental feeler or antenna, which goes out sensitively and explores the terrain, as if, before the actual execution of the technique, one were to perform it in imagination first.

In Chinese, the character 'I' is often translated as 'mind'; a better translation might be 'will' or 'intention'. In the T'ai Chi classics, it is said:

'The intention directs the ch'i
The ch'i directs the body.'

The skill consists in not trying to use the body directly, with brute muscular force; first use the will to direct the energy, forming a clear, sensitive feeling of the movement, then let the physical movement follow.

The strong will

This is the aspect of the will which is most easily distorted. In the martial arts there is naturally the need for power, and a great deal may be at stake, so there will often be considerable pressure for success. The impulse is strong to tense the muscles, grit the teeth, and generally act unskilfully. Often the effort goes into the arms, shoulders, face and upper body generally; but the true source of power, and the residence of the strong will, is in the lower body. The abdomen, lower back, thighs and calves contain the strongest muscles, and a well-developed awareness in this region is the basis for an inner feeling of power and strength. What is more, the lower body links the upper body to the ground; and it is the ground itself from which all power to act ultimately comes. Try pushing a car while wearing roller skates and you'll see what I mean. Only through firm contact with the ground can the muscles find a foundation from which to act.

To refer to 'the lower body' generally as the seat of power, while true in a way, is rather vague. The most important thing in the strong will is that the whole self should be behind the decision, in an integrated way, with all parts acting together. Thus in the body we need to find that place which gathers and masses all the forces of the body. That point is known in Japanese as *seika-no-itten*, or 'the one point in the lower abdomen'. It corresponds approximately to the physical centre of gravity of the body, and is located about three fingerwidths (1½ in.; 4 cm.) below the navel. It is actually in the middle of the body, closer to the back than to the front in a ratio of 3:7, which puts it roughly at the centre of the intervertebral disc between the third and fourth lumbar vertebrae. Because of its proximity to the centre of gravity and its particular anatomical location, this is the gathering point for all the power of the body, the place where mind and body can meet most intimately. This point is well known in the Far and Near East, and both it and the area around it (the lower abdomen) are often referred to as the centre for unification, power, bodily movement and stability. It is the 'earth centre' of the body, which relates the body to the earth and allows the power of the earth to be gathered up into the pelvis and then relayed out, as the mind directs, to arms and hands.

Natural breathing while focussing on this spot can increase the power stored here. In many martial arts, the student must make a habit of keeping his attention at 'the one point'. In this state, any action undertaken will be backed by the totality of the person's physical and spiritual resources, and the act of will acquires strength as well as skill.

The good will

This aspect of will raises the question of value, or what all this skill and strength is to be used for. The ethical questions of the martial arts are thrown into prominence. Westbrook and Ratti describe a variety of uses of power in the martial arts, ranging in degree of ethicality. The lowest level is that of unprovoked violent attack; little better is the goading of another into attack and then defending oneself violently. All martial arts would agree in condemning such behaviour. Intermediate is a code espoused by many external systems: do not provoke attack, indeed do all you can to avoid it. But if you can no longer avoid it, retaliate with total power: kill with one blow.

Many internal martial arts adopt a more moderate ethic, similar to the Old Testament doctrine of 'an eye for an eye, a tooth for a tooth'. Rather than responding with total violence or not at all, the response is graduated to the attack, as if the attacker's own energy were returned back to him. A soft shove is countered by a soft shove, a hard punch by a hard punch, a death blow by a death blow.

But the highest level is found in Aikido, which truly shows what the good will can be in terms of the martial arts. In Aikido, the aim is always to defend yourself or others without harming your opponent. The spirit is one of universal love. The words of the great Master, O-Sensei Uyeshiba, express the deepest level of good will, the highest ethic of the martial arts

Aiki is not a technique to fight with or defeat the enemy. It is the way to reconcile the world and make human beings one family. . . .

There is no enemy for Uyeshiba of Aikido. You are mistaken if you think that *budo* [spiritually oriented martial art] means to have opponents and enemies and to be strong and fell them. There are neither opponents nor enemies for true *budo*. True *budo* is to be one with the universe; that is, to be united with the Centre of the universe.

This is not only the highest ethic, but also the key to the most effective technique in the martial arts. To quote Uyeshiba again,

The secret of Aikido is to harmonize ourselves with the movement of the universe and bring ourselves into accord with the universe itself. He who has gained the secret of Aikido has the universe in himself and can say, 'I am the universe'.

I am never defeated, however fast the enemy may attack. It is not because my technique is faster than that of the enemy. It is not a question of speed. The fight is finished before it is begun.

When an enemy tries to fight with me, the universe itself, he has to break the harmony of the universe. Hence at the moment he has the mind to fight with me, he is already defeated. There is no measure of time – fast or slow.

Aikido is non-resistance. As it is non-resistant, it is always victorious.

What more perfect expression of Christ's doctrine –

Ye have heard that it hath been said, An eye for an eye, and a tooth for a tooth: But I say unto you, that ye resist not evil: but whatsoever shall smite thee on thy right cheek, turn to him the other also. (Matthew 6:38,39).

If the heart is open and pure, there is no place for harm to enter; and at the deepest level, love and will are one.

3   Body, energy, mind and spirit

Body – Breath – Mind

This basic trilogy occurs throughout teachings on spirituality and the martial arts, and refers to certain universal laws. It relates closely to the three principles (Head-Heart-Belly) explained in the first section, but emphasizes the dynamic interplay between these three, and describes the nature of the creative process involved in all of life, from a simple movement to the painting of the Sistine Chapel. Body, Breath and Mind are three different forms of energy which coexist in the person and his universe.

The Body relates to the Belly principle, and its centre is the *hara*, the region around 'the one point'. It is physical form, substance, sensation, the actual physical structure of our body or of any object. It also includes the 'subtle body', which is a sort of condensation from our past actions and attitudes, and which surrounds and penetrates our body like a restricting, crystallized energy field.

The Breath relates to the Heart principle; but here two provisos should be stated. First, each principle, as manifested in a person's body, contains within itself the other two also; so the pelvic area is not the *exclusive* domain of the Belly principle, nor the chest area that of the Heart principle.

Second, the Heart principle has two distinct levels. The more superficial places it as a third principle between two others: thought-emotion-sensation, or Mind-Breath-Body. But at a deeper level the Heart transcends and embraces the other two, as rhythm embraces beat and pause, as intuition embraces thought, emotion and sensation. The Heart in its more limited sense relates to the throat and solar plexus; in its deeper sense, to the heart area itself.

So Breath relates particularly to the throat. This includes the physical breath, but also the emotions, which are so closely connected to breathing. This level of energy has a flowing, dynamic quality unlike the fixity of the Body level. It is colourful, moving, active, and is strongly involved in 'relating'; it is the energy of attraction or repulsion, the flow of the emotions.

The Mind energy level is the most subtle and non-physical; it is the essence. It is the level of pure awareness, of understanding, choice and intention. It relates, of course, to the Head principle, and its centre is at the third eye or the crown of the head. Thought, as we normally experience it, is really a symptom of contraction or congestion on this energy level; unconstrained, it has a subtle, open, timeless quality of awareness and bright intention which does not split into 'observer' and 'thing observed'.

These three energy levels (Body, Breath and Mind) are always in dynamic interaction, and for true health they should all be balanced with each other. This balance and integration has its centre in the heart area, and corresponds (as mentioned above) to the Heart principle in its wider sense.

The use of these interacting levels in practice may be understood through an analogy. Body is matter, solid, like rocks. Breath is like water, flowing and powerful; Mind is like air, pervasive and open. The Western philosophical viewpoint, regarding mind and matter (or body) as the two major aspects of reality, is confronted with the mind/body problem. How can the mind, such an ethereal and abstract entity, cause movement in something so solid and tangible as a physical body? Where the link should be, an enormous gulf as between two separate universes seems to loom. How can the gentle wind blow the solid rocks around? The logical answer is, it has to try very hard – hence the whole doctrine of effort: if at first you don't succeed, try, try again. Implicitly, try harder than before, make more effort; the whole way you approach the problem is not questioned.

An experiment bearing on this attitude was done by a running coach; his trainees were asked to make an all-out, total effort at the mile run, and their performance times were recorded. Then, a short while later, they were asked to make the same run at three-quarters effort: interestingly, they all made better speeds the second time.

The Eastern approach begins, not with the assumption of a basic body/mind split, but with the attitude that the universe is a whole. Within that whole, different aspects can be seen, as any complex shape looks different when seen from different points of view. The main different aspects are Body, Breath and Mind. No problem exists in principle when considering how Mind affects Body; the energy movement flows from one level to the next. The wind blows on the water, raising waves, creating currents; the water rolls boulders around with ease. The Mind directs the Breath, the Breath moves the Body. The Mind intends and chooses the motion, sets up the direction for the energy flow. Then the feeling-energy flows out, and finally carries the physical body along the same pathway.

This may be seen to perfection in a cat jumping onto a ledge. There is no struggle or effort, no anxious preparation. Rather, the animal first sees the ledge, orients to it, decides to jump. Then the gaze flows out to the ledge as the body crouches, settling into itself a little; one has the impression that the spirit and energy of the cat are already on the ledge, only the body remaining behind. Then, with an ease suggesting an afterthought, the cat's body uncoils and rejoins its spirit up on the ledge.

A simple exercise, known in Aikido as 'The Unbendable Arm', may clarify this principle in terms of its practical application.

For this experiment, you need a sympathetic partner of about your own strength. Stand opposite each other; raise your right arm comfortably, parallel to the floor, fist clenched. Let your partner grip your wrist with his or her right hand and, holding your elbow with his left, let him try to bend your arm at the elbow by forcing your fist towards your face. He should gradually put all his strength into this effort, without sudden jerks, and you should make your greatest effort to stop him and keep your arm straight.

If you are fairly well matched in strength, your partner will succeed in bending your arm (his two arms being pitted against your one) without excessive effort. Now, stop and relax, shaking your arm out thoroughly (as described on p. 12). Shake your arm until it tingles. Raise and lower it a few times, fingers pointing out, and feel the movement. Then relax, and *imagine* the same raising and lowering as vividly as possible. The aim is to imagine the *feeling* of the movement. Then repeat the actual raising together with the imagining (all of which activates the arm's energy field), and point towards something in the distance. Imagine your arm to be a firehose, through which a powerful stream of water is gushing, far into the distance. Let all your thought and feeling be with this image, without tense effort. As you prepare, let your partner assume the same position as before, ready to try bending your arm. When he senses you to be well settled in the image, he should begin trying to bend your arm, building up pressure gradually without jerks, until he is trying at least as hard as before. You ignore his efforts, all your attention being absorbed in the image of extension.

You will find that not only does your partner find it much more difficult, if not impossible, to bend your arm this second time, but also that you have little or no sense of effort in keeping your arm straight (in contrast to the struggle of the first time). By choosing (Mind) to energize the image of extension (Breath), the derived state of your arm (Body) comes about with ease.

This principle can be applied to almost any human activity, physical, emotional or mental. I leave it to the reader's ingenuity to discover some of these applications in his or her own life.

The integration of the structure of Breath and Body

From the preceding discussion, it should be clear that Breath and Body are vital to the pursuit of both spiritual unfoldment and the mastery of the martial arts. It is vital to understand the basic structure of Breath and Body accurately and in detail. This understanding may be gained intuitively in the presence of a true master over a long period of time; this has been the traditional way of teaching. This way requires a certain natural capacity on the part of the student. T'ai Chi Master Cheng Man-Ch'ing once said that the mastery of T'ai Chi depended on a certain head balance. But, he said, there is no way of teaching it; you either have it, and thus have the potential to master T'ai Chi, or you don't have it.

Now the fact is that, in our current technological society, we are in much, much worse shape physically than are members of traditional cultures. I am not speaking of freedom from such things as infectious diseases or malnutrition, nor of muscular strength or endurance, but of basic good body alignment, balanced muscular tonus and natural, full breathing. In these terms, compared with our own past or with other traditional societies, we are in a truly appalling condition. 'Malposture', as Professor Raymond Dart has called it, is by far the most widespread disorder in the

West, and a survey conducted for the White House Conference for Child Health reported that 80% or more of American children had bad body mechanics. And by this I do not mean some deportment-school model of Victorian uprightness, but a natural litheness and freedom of movement. With this material to work with, even the traditional master has a hard time. Sensei K. Chiba, a high-ranking Aikido master who taught in London for many years, used to shout at his Western pupils, in frustration, 'more lightly! more lightly!', not knowing how to instil that basic integration which most Japanese have naturally.

In the Chinese internal martial arts, we have some of the most explicit descriptions of this basic bodily poise. Many instructions are given: to 'straighten the neck', and 'let the waist sink', to 'depress the chest' and 'hollow the groin'. These instructions can be heard, interpreted, carried out, but in the end it seems an astonishingly difficult job for anything to result from all this other than a new set of postural distortions. I have seen this happen many times. I don't mean to say it is inevitable, but it is very common indeed.

Fortunately, in each culture teachings arise to suit the precise needs of that culture, and in the West we have the work of F. Matthias Alexander. His approach, the Alexander Technique, is very hard to describe in a short space, and I would refer those interested to his writings or, better, to lessons with a qualified teacher. Much of the following is based on insights from Alexander's work; it is not to be taken directly as a description of his technique, but owes a very large debt to the teachings of this remarkable man.

In Alexander's analysis of the problems of contemporary man we find echoes of teachings from many sources; certainly he is saying with great clarity what many martial arts masters have difficulty expressing (at least in contemporary Western terms); and we can also relate his teachings to those of Zen Buddhism and Taoism. Indeed, almost all spiritual systems emphasize the importance of a 'straight spine', especially in sitting meditation. And in Alexander's teachings we have a modern analysis of what this 'straight spine' constitutes and what its importance is.

Firstly, as has been stressed earlier, the bodily position is not important in itself. More fundamental is the poise, or dynamic balance of the body; the underlying tonus of the body tissue. A 'straight' spine held rigid through muscular contraction may have a superficial resemblance to a lightly poised 'natural' spine, but there is clearly a fundamental difference. In the naturally poised body no muscle is fixed rigidly or flaccid and collapsed. Throughout, there is an alive balance between tension and relaxation (sometimes referred to as 'eutony', in contrast to 'hypertony' and 'hypotony').

But more importantly, this bodily state is not merely a physical state; it is rather a condition of the whole person, of his Self; this is why Alexander called one of his books *The Use of the Self*. This is also why the Zen Buddhists can say: 'When sitting correctly in Za-Zen one is not practising towards becoming the Buddha; while sitting correctly, one *is* the Buddha.'

The natural poise, while basically *one* condition, has various aspects, each of which may be described in external and internal terms.

The neck is free, and the head floats lightly, poised at its highest natural stature. Thus the mind is clear, the awareness is free and wide like someone surveying a vast, open plain. In other words, the awareness is not introverted, constricted or fixed on any one thing (all of which would involve tightening the neck and pulling the head back and down). The Chinese describe this as 'the spirit rises to the top of the head'.

The spine, and the whole of the back, are long, elastic and free. The lower back is not tight or hollowed; as the neck springs upwards, the tailbone lengthens downwards, creating a resilience throughout the back. The Chinese speak of 'raising the back' and 'sinking the loins'. In other words, the whole self is knit in a flexible unity, giving a sense of firmness, of connection, of oneness. The tail releasing down establishes roots in the Earth, the solid ground of one's Being; the neck releasing up allows the growth of the person towards the spiritual Sun of full consciousness.

Not only is the back long, but it also widens, giving rise to an easy expansive breadth. The shoulders widen and are neither slumped nor held rigidly back; the ribs float easily out from the spine, creating space within, and neither collapse nor are held rigidly inflated; the lower back broadens, making a powerful base for connection into the legs. This is complementary to the lengthening of the back; too much lengthening without widening creates a narrow attitude of arrogant spiritual aspiration. The widening adds an expansive attitude which moves out into the world, towards other people and the life of the Earth. The Heart is the centre of this expansion, and love is its essence.

The limbs are integrated with the trunk so that the hands and feet are in intimate relation to the body core. This tends to come about as the core body poise improves, and necessitates a freeing of the limb joints so that the limbs become light and responsive to the impulses from the centre. Thus the pathways are opened for full contact with and action on the world, the capacity to reach out and touch other people and the earth, to form and be formed by what is without.

As a natural result of the restoration of poise, the breathing process is freed. Chest, abdomen, back, and indeed the whole body, become able to participate; the freezing, which prevents breathing from permeating the different parts, melts. Breathing is no longer a tense heaving of chest and shoulders or a limited expansion of the abdomen, nor a self-conscious filling of different parts in turn, but a subtle, powerful flow which continuously energizes and cleanses every cell of the body. This involves a continual willingness to take in from, and to give out to, the environment; neither creating an impenetrable boundary which bars contact, nor losing all sense of self through a slack dissolution of boundaries. Again we see the Middle Way, the balance of yin and yang in the flow of Tao.

The above conditions form the basic background; naturally each martial art may require certain postures which appear to deviate from these fundamentals (as the boxer pulls his chin down and raises his shoulders to protect it, or the *karateka* creates tremendous contraction in his muscles to 'focus' a blow). But unless this natural, open condition is present as the matrix for all action and awareness, any specific skill becomes a trap and, instead of being mastered, becomes the master.

What I say applies also to meditative disciplines. Tibetan Buddhism employs many elaborate visualizations; but before and after such practices, the basic, open, unfixed state of mind is invoked. Hatha Yoga develops complex and powerful techniques of breath control; but unless natural breathing already exists as a background to such disciplines, they can be very damaging and may create further layers of obstruction to free functioning.

These ABCs are all too often neglected by those who want to run before they can crawl.

Rhythm, power and freedom

The nervous system integrates body, breath and mind into a single unit. A basic characteristic of this unity is vibration or pulsation, which may be seen on all levels of organization. Vibration is shown in the brain waves recorded on an electroencephalogram, in the activity of the nerves, the peristaltic rhythms, muscle action, body movement patterns, and so on. In fact vibration is the basic building block of the universe, creating the elementary particles and their interactions, giving rise to the atomic and molecular levels, and guiding the formation of complex cellular structures.

Any vibration has certain basic properties, such as rhythm (or frequency); power (or amplitude); and character (or waveform). The frequency of a vibration is its rate of pulsation, or how many times a second it vibrates; the amplitude simply means how large the vibrations are; and waveform refers to the particular shape of the vibration. This last is generated by several vibrations acting together; a single vibration ('pure tone') has one particular shape called a 'sine curve'. But if several frequencies act together they can create a combined vibration with quite a different shape or character.

Rhythms interact with each other in various ways; they may be consonant or dissonant. Two consonant or harmonious sounds have a mutually reinforcing effect, and their respective frequencies will be even multiples or simple fractions of each other; whereas dissonant or unharmonious sounds have a mutually destructive effect and their frequencies are not even multiples. (This may be illustrated easily by playing on the piano the notes c, C, G, and G'; and then the notes c, f# or C, C#. Careful listening will reveal the interference beats in the latter two pairs.)

When two vibratory systems are harmonious they tend to resonate together, as when a plucked guitar string vibrates an adjacent string tuned to the same note. This condition of resonance allows transfer and communication of energy between the two (or more) components of the system. The television aerial and the tuning of a radio are examples of applied resonance. In the television aerial, it is its particular length and shape that allows it to resonate with (pick up) the television frequencies of electromagnetic waves while resonating very weakly or not at all with radio frequencies. Similarly, tuning a radio to a particular station involves changing the length of a piece of metal in the receiver so that it resonates with the desired frequency.

Another important vibratory phenomenon is that of 'entrainment'. If two linked vibrating systems have similar but not identical frequencies (i.e. not resonant), then they will gradually tend to come closer together in frequency until they are the same (resonant). That is, one frequency (usually the fastest) entrains the other, bringing it up to the same speed. When this happens and the two are in resonance, energy can begin to pass back and forth between them. For instance, if there are two pendulums hanging from a wire, and one is swinging at 7 cycles per second and the other at $6\frac{1}{2}$ cycles per second, then gradually the latter will speed up until they are both at 7 cps. Then an interesting thing happens: one of the pendulums begins to swing more strongly (though still at the same frequency) and the other less strongly until one is still and the other has all the power of both. Then the process reverses itself, and so on, as the energy of vibration is passed back and forth between the two resonant pendulums.

All these facts of physics have a strong bearing on the functioning of the living organism, its capacity to function in an integrated way and to tune in to different levels of spiritual experience. All the rhythms of the being interact with each other, forming an incredibly complex vibratory network, a bit like the entrancing patterns created by the ripples of a handful of stones thrown into a still pool. An organism in which the various rhythms are relatively harmonious does not lose energy in dissonant beats, and the different parts are in good communication through sympathetic resonance.

Different states of conflict or harmony have their corresponding vibratory pattern, and these vibratory patterns entail a resonant communication with other beings and energies of similar vibratory pattern. Thus if a person is in a state of anger and inner conflict, he will emit relatively disharmonious vibrations, and these will put him in communication with people and events of a similar (angry, dissonant) pattern. This will tend to draw such situations to him, and he will begin to experience in his external world events similar in feeling to those going on inside him. (Notice, however, that this theory really denies any basic separation between the internal and external world.)

This process occurs partly through quite subtle energy levels, but an important aspect is the more obvious one of physical movement, both micromovements and gross movement.

Recent research into micromovements (very small rhythmic motions of the body) has shown that they alter consistently and dramatically with different emotional and meditative states. Manfred Clynes, in his work on Sentics, demonstrates that micromovements of the fingers correspond to the major emotions; for example, anger is a sharp movement away from the body, grief is a slow heavy downward motion and joy a smooth, light, lifting movement. Clynes presents evidence that the voluntary adoption of these movement patterns tends to bring on the corresponding feeling; and Ostrander and Schroeder report that Russian scientists have detected similar phenomena and have succeeded in broadcasting these vibrations by electromagnetic waves, so that emotions such as fear and anger can be induced *at a distance* in an unsuspecting subject.

Lee Sanella, in his fascinating little book *Kundalini: Psychosis or Transcendence?*, tells us that if one measures the random movements of the top of a person's head as they sit in meditation, one can tell how advanced they are; the head of a mature Zen meditator hardly moves, whereas a novice's wobbles all over the place.

In the same book, Sanella presents fascinating evidence concerning Kundalini meditation (which brings about a process of physical and mental cleansing by activating the inner healing power). It seems that the crucial factor in this process is a series of resonances and entrainments of bodily rhythms around the root frequency of 7 cps. Starting with the aorta (the main artery, in the centre of the body) the following resonances are entrained: the whole body, the brain, the brain ventricles, the cerebrospinal fluid, circular electrical currents in the cortex, and the electromagnetic field surrounding the head. This last in turn resonates with the fields of others in a similar meditative state, and finally resonates with the electro-magnetic field of the atmosphere whose frequency is also, amazingly enough, 7 cps.

Dance therapists are familiar with the way that movement reflects the inner being, and with the way that change in movement can encourage a change in the inner feelings. Penny Bernstein has even made a study of movement patterns in terms of the Freudian character types. Oral, anal and genital types all have their typical gestures. And David Boadella and David Smith have begun integrating the work of Penny Bernstein, Rudolf Laban, Wilhelm Reich and others into a comprehensive theory of psychological types that is firmly based on the body's capacities for rhythmic, vibratory movement.

It should be remembered, as has been stressed previously, that there is in reality no 'outer' and 'inner' self which affect each other. There is but one self, though one may perceive it from different sides, and in different degrees of subtlety. Between thought, feeling and movement there is no absolute division; thought seen from the outside is movement, movement from the inside is feeling. Movement, being the more visible, tangible and volitional aspect of one's being, often may be more easily modified. Modify the movement towards integration, harmony and power, and by gradual rhythmic entrainment the rest of the being will follow. In truth, the initial modification of movement will not be accurate, but merely the imitation of the desired movement; not until the whole being vibrates to the same chord will the motion be true. But the imitation, especially continuous imitation in the presence of a master of the desired state, will (by the medium of resonance and rhythmic entrainment) gradually bring about the transformation.

In the traditional teaching of T'ai Chi, this is indeed the procedure. The master stands in front of his students and allows the movements of his body to express his inner being through the form. The circular, rhythmic movements are like a river, a tree in motion, peaceful and silent as the run rising, powerful as a stalking leopard, as empty of self-preoccupation as a blade of grass. And the students fumble their way through their empty simulations. The demands of the movements, the palpable presence of the master, make them painfully aware of their physical stiffness, their emotional restrictions, their grasping thoughts. With this awareness comes self-knowledge and humility. And gradually the dissonances are smoothed out, the contractions undone, and the resonance between master and student begins to allow communication on a level beyond words and imitation. The freedom and emptiness of the master communes with the silence within each soul, coaxing openness into openness.

In all martial arts teaching (as in all movement systems), great attention is paid to detail in posture and gesture. This is not because what is desired is a certain precise technique; rather the master's correction says to the student 'if your spirit were in the right state it would manifest in your movement, and it would be *thus*'. What is important is the spirit, which can manifest in an infinite variety of movements; but equally there are infinite movements that do *not* express it. And even an apparently correct movement without the spirit behind it will miss the mark in myriad subtle ways. A correction by the master may indicate this missing of the mark even if the external form is apparently correct.

The above explanation deals with T'ai Chi in particular, but it conveys the principles behind body movement systems in general as means towards spiritual change. In other martial arts different qualities may be stressed, such as one-pointedness (focussed concentration), speed or determination, but the principles outlined above remain valid regardless of the particular nature of the communication. In Hatha Yoga, for instance, the *asana* (or posture), with its precise bodily positioning, acts as a resonant antenna for certain forms of energy which may be communicated across time as well as space. It is said that in each *asana* a yogin attained enlightenment; through entering into the essence of the *asana* the practitioner will attain communion with the energy of this enlightened being.

Body movement and awareness:
the key to the psychophysical energy of *ki*

There is no space here for a comprehensive treatment of the psychophysical energy known in Japanese as *ki*. But a few words are essential in any treatment of the martial arts, especially in a book directed at Westerners. It is a peculiar fact that our culture is one of the few in the history of the world which has no everyday word or concept corresponding to *ki*. This might be argued as being due to the rise of science which has more 'accurate' concepts than these 'vague, vitalistic ideas'. But if this were so, one would expect science to be conversant with and capable of dealing effectively with those areas in which *ki* is usually invoked. These areas include basic vitality, mental and emotional health, intuition, body-mind relationships, paranormal powers, as well as the extraordinary capacities already described which can be attained by masters of *ki*. Clearly science has an almost total lack of competence in these, and related areas.

Some recent claims have been made for the equivalence of certain recent scientific discoveries and *ki*; for instance, the Kirlian aura evidenced when 'photographing' an object in a high frequency electromagnetic field. But while the Kirlian aura, like many other phenomena such as blood circulation, skin colour, body temperature, electromagnetic and electrostatic fields and micromovement vibrations, shows fluctuation with the subject's energy state, there is no basis for jumping to the conclusion that this aura *is* the *ki*.

The word for *ki* in different cultures usually carries implications of both 'breath' and 'spirit', linking the material and the immaterial. (Indeed the Latin word *spiritus* also means 'breath', a connection still present in our words 'expire' and 'inspire', both of which have double meanings.) In Greek, the word is *pneuma*; in Sanskrit, *prana*, in Chinese, *ch'i*; in Polynesian, *mana*; in Hebrew, *ruach*, in Bushmen *n/um* (where the / represents a click). Recently in the West various people have developed this concept, though none have been accepted into mainstream Western consciousness. Anton Mesmer's 'magnetic fluid', Von Reichenbach's 'Odic force', and Wilhelm Reich's 'Orgone energy' all deal with *ki*.

Ki is an energy which is inherently linked with life and consciousness, and which can produce direct effects on physical energies and matter. Indeed, the action of *ki* is often associated with electrical and magnetic effects, which seem to be side-effects rather than the main active principles. *Ki* can be directed by conscious intention. *Ki* moves like smoke, like water; it flows, has coherence and pattern, yet is unfixed and formless. It can be generated and accumulated in the body to increase the overall capacity for all forms of action or experience. Its effects can be felt in the body as sensations of heat and cold, lightness and heaviness, smoothness and roughness, expansion and contraction, and so on. On an emotional level it corresponds to the Freudian 'libido'. When being consciously developed, it is often first felt in the hands as warmth, tingling and heaviness. The hands may feel as though they are moving through a magnetic field; when held close together, as if holding a ball, and moved very slightly, a 'magnetic field' may be felt between them. This is not literally a magnetic field as a physicist uses the word, but is what Mesmer called 'animal magnetism'; the *ki* field. With further practice the *ki* begins to be felt in the arms, the legs and throughout the body. It may also be felt round the body, between oneself and other people or things at a distance. It becomes a new mode of perception and action; or rather a conscious rediscovery of the basic, original mode. One's own flow of *ki* can be felt and consciously directed within and around the body; it will normally influence the flow of *ki* in and around other people or things; and when very powerfully developed it can strongly affect mental states and physical movement at a distance, enabling psychokinesis and telepathic hypnosis.

The *ki* is developed through conscious linking of physical movement, breathing and focussed attention. In many *ki*-development exercises, the body (its correct poise assumed) is moved in easy, fluid patterns which harmonize with the natural motions of the musculo-skeletal structure and with the flow of *ki* (these are in fact largely identical, since the flow patterns of *ki* were the template for the condensation of the body's physical structure). The rhythm of the breath is allowed to link with the movement, and the mind is called into play by imagining the breath as the flow of *ki* (which may be visualized as a golden fluid) through and beyond the body parts involved in the movement. The awareness is concentrated without tension, fully open to the whole field of action. Naturally the actual performance of such exercises can only be learned through direct personal instruction.

The *ki* thus developed may be stored, usually in the *hara*, or lower abdomen and pelvis, and may be directed at will to whatever task is undertaken. Many healing methods use the direction of *ki* to the affected part as a means of catalysing the body's own processes to restore proper functioning. The artist directs his *ki* into the movements of the brush, the warrior into the sword.

Just as electricity comes both as high voltage, low current energy (as in high-voltage lines, in which it can travel for miles with little power expenditure), and as low voltage, high current house energy (which can turn an electric fire element red-hot), so *ki* comes in different 'currents' and 'voltages'; the 'low voltage, high current' kind having much stronger physical effects and the 'high voltage, low current' kind being much more 'ethereal' and more linked with pure spirit and transcendent experiences. So, as well as the task of accumulating the *ki*, there is also the process of 'refining' it, raising its 'voltage' and establishing connections to more expanded, penetrative levels of consciousness.

The ego structure and the body

One last point concerning the importance of the body in spiritual matters.

Freud said, 'the ego is a body ego'. The nature of the ego, the ordinary sense of 'I', is intimately bound up with the physical body. Death itself is equated with the loss of the body. And those who have no fear of death because they believe in reincarnation or an afterlife are consoled by the idea of future resumption of a new body, or of continued existence in a subtler 'body'. Our whole sense of *who* we are, and, even deeper, *that* we are, is based in our body sensations and body image.

We have previously discussed the relation between parts of the body and 'parts' of the psyche; but the whole sense of *being* an ego, separate from the world about us, is based on our ordinary bodily experience. We usually feel our bodies as separate, ending at the surface of our skin; and, concomitantly, we feel the world as 'out there', as 'not us', connected with ourselves only indirectly. This is the fundamental condition of most of us, this separation, and may be the root of all suffering.

Both science and mysticism agree that this experience of things is not absolute and true, but relative, arbitrary and illusory. Modern physics asserts that we are actually made up of curved, empty space, and that no absolute boundary can be detected between 'self' and 'world'; our space is continuous with that of the world, like 'water flowing into water'.

Neurophysiology supports this view. It is now known that the visual system, for instance, does not operate like a camera, 'photographing' a more or less accurate picture of some independent 'external world'. Rather, our visual experience is the result of a complex set of creative operations which build up in our awareness, from moment to moment, a consistent image which we take to be 'the world'. But in fact this image derives from patterns of activity in the neurones of our brain; and the relation of these patterns to the qualities of actual conscious experience is a profound mystery. It is clear at any rate that we are certainly not 'seeing the world' in the way we normally think we are.

Similarly, one's body sensations and body image are built up in the brain; the body image is probably created in the right parietal lobe of the cortex. Thus we have precisely the same relation to our 'inner' world as to the 'outer' one. But, also in our brain, the category of 'spatial experience' is developed, and certain things come to be experienced as 'outside' and 'inside'. 'Space', 'insideness' and 'outsideness' do not exist as 'external' facts. They are created experiences within consciousness. This obviously turns our normal view of things inside-out: if space itself is created by 'mind', then where is mind? If 'insideness' and 'outsideness' are created in the brain, then is the brain 'inside' the skull? Is the 'world' 'inside' or 'outside' the brain? All these questions seem to dissolve and become meaningless as a vastly wider perspective opens up, in which the usual distinctions between body and mind, self and world, become relative and somewhat arbitrary. The idea and experience of ourselves as 'being' one and 'not being' the other is something set up by us, usually under the influence of cultural conditioning, and has no absolute or unalterable validity. As Carlos Castaneda's teacher says, we 'do' the world, and we can stop doing it and let it dissolve back into the ungraspable reality prior to self and world.

With the development and expansion of *ki*, the feelings of 'inside-outside' begin to alter, and one's relationship with the world becomes more intimate, boundaries become permeable, and the distinction between self and opponent becomes less fixed. In the higher stages of Aikido, combat becomes a harmonious dance of exquisite beauty. Listen to the words of Uyeshiba describing his enlightenment out of which Aikido was created:

Then in the spring of 1925, if I remember correctly, when I was taking a walk in the garden by myself, I felt that a golden spirit sprang up from the ground, veiled my body and changed my body into a golden one.

At the same time my mind and body turned into light. I was able to understand the whispering of the birds, and was clearly aware of the mind of God, the Creator of this universe.

At that moment I was enlightened: the source of *budo* is God's love – the spirit of loving protection for all beings. Endless tears of joy streamed down my cheeks. Since that time I have grown to feel that the whole earth is my house, and the sun, the moon and the stars are all my own things.

The training of *budo* is to take God's love, which correctly produces, protects and cultivates all things in Nature, and assimilate and utilize it in our own mind and body.

With full attainment, the narrow sense of self dissolves. The realization is born that consciousness does not belong to anyone; there is no one for it to belong to. Consciousness is not 'it' but 'I'; the 'universal I' which creates space and time and is the nature of all things: consciousness, existence, love.

Then, how can you straighten your warped mind, purify your heart, and be harmonized with the activities of all things in Nature? You should first make God's heart yours. It is a Great Love, Omnipresent in all quarters and in all times of the universe. 'There is no discord in love. There is no enemy of love'. A mind of discord, thinking of the existence of an enemy, is no more consistent with the will of God.

Morihei Uyeshiba

Master Nakano, dressed in ceremonial robes, practising Kyudo ('The Way of the Bow') in his garden.

The mind, or intention, goes forth and becomes one with the target. There is thus no self-conscious effort to aim at and hit the target; indeed, such effort implies the likelihood of error. Since the archer is at one with both bow and target, the arrow has no distance to travel; missing becomes impossible, even self-contradictory.

Two aspects of the founder of Aikido, O-Sensei Morihei Uyeshiba. On the left, in an attitude of Shinto prayer; on the right, uttering the *kiai* as he simultaneously evades and counters a sword-blow from Tamura-Sensei.

Most martial arts, in their deeper aspects, manifest seemingly paradoxical extremes of human capacity. From the depths of devotional prayer comes an openness and freedom of spirit, which can allow a precise, spontaneous and total surging forth of power. In the right-hand picture, O-Sensei combines leonine ferocity with measured precision as he tucks his left arm out of the way of the descending sword, at the same time striking his attacker with the fan in his right hand.

In most religious systems, the archetypes of the warrior/slayer/weapon wielder have a position of prominence. The principle of destruction, so essential to the creative process, may be embodied as a ferocious demon. Insight, which cuts through the confusion of mind – as when Alexander the Great severed the Gordian Knot – can be symbolized as wielding a razor-sharp sword. And the spiritual power which overcomes the little devils of doubt and ignorance, and which gives the practitioner the inner strength to transmute his neuroses into forces for growth, is manifested in the collective imagination as a powerful, warrior-like figure.

Here are portrayed two such beings: on the left, Mahakala, the Tibetan god of power and destruction; and on the right, Shoki the Demon-queller, a Japanese adaptation of a Chinese deity (note the characteristic straight Chinese sword) who is widely invoked as talisman against negative states of mind. (Tanka, Tibet, 18th–19th c.; the actor Nakamura Utaemon IV as Shoki the Demon-queller, print by Sadonobu, Japan, 1838.)

Son of the founder of Aikido and its present head, Aikido Doshu Kisshomaru Uyeshiba-sensei (right) performs a masterful 'four-side throw' from a seated position against a standing opponent (*shiho-nage hanmi-handachi*). His immense calm and balance in the midst of whirling movement is reflected in the fan painting of a seaweed

gatherer deftly poised amid the
power of the ocean. The motions of
Aikido, of all the martial arts, show
the resonances with the natural
movements of wind and water. (Fan
painting by Sadahide, Japan, c. 1850;
photo of Uyeshiba-sensei taken
during his first visit to England,
under the sponsorship of the British
Aikido Federation, 1975.)

The name 'T'ai Chi Ch'uan', an ancient and profound Chinese martial art, is impossible to translate literally. It has been rendered as 'Great Ultimate Boxing', 'Grand Terminus Fist' and 'Primordial Pugilism'. The words 'T'ai Chi' refer to the yin-yang diagram in which the interflowing black and white shapes symbolize the fundamental positive and negative forces of the universe; forces which are not in polar antagonism but which, in their cooperative and complementary dance, generate all the phenomena of the universe (as winter and summer produce the year, inspiration and expiration breathing, and male and female the new human). The word 'Ch'uan' means 'fist', and refers both to the physical body generally and to combat in particular. So 'T'ai Chi Ch'uan' means a system of combat which manifests, through the physical body, the fundamental yin-yang laws of the universe.

As such, its movements are simple and natural, as shown in this photo of Patty Parmalee performing the movement *tao nien hou* ('Step Back and Repulse Monkey'). (Ms Parmalee is a T'ai Chi instructor at the Aspen Academy of the Martial Arts (P.O.B. 1939, Aspen, Colorado), a centre which aims to create an environment for intense and disciplined study of a number of martial arts.)

The movements of T'ai Chi are reflected in the photo of two Nuba wrestlers from Sudan; the natural pattern of one hand high and forward, the other back and low, is seen in both photographs.

Types of weapon use evolve in relation to the natural and most efficient ways of moving the body. Despite stylistic and technical differences, the resonances can be seen between this picture of an early 18th-century Italian fencing academy, in which people can be seen training in the use of one- and two-handed swords, knives, staves and halberds, and the modern photograph of a confrontation between the traditional Japanese arts of Kendo, 'The Way of the Sword', and Jo-jitsu, 'The Technique of the Staff', where the weapon is the *jo*, or 4-ft-long (1.2 m.) oak staff. Note the similarity between the technique of the left-hand figure in the foreground of the Italian print and that of the Jo-jitsu combatant in the photograph.

In all martial arts, footwork is of fundamental importance. On the left, a banner illustrating Karate foot movements; and on the right, the warrior Matsuomaru wielding an axe, feet powerfully braced for the blow. The traditional split skirt, or *hakama*, of the Samurai, still worn by Aikido black belts, was designed to conceal one's footwork from the opponent without interfering with freedom of movement. (Banner by John Dugger, England, 20th c.; the actor Ichikawa Danjuro VII as Matsuomaru, print by Kunisada, Japan, c. 1836.)

The martial arts are by no means an exclusively male province. On the left, Masae Hayashi, a Karate black belt, demonstrates a strongly focussed left *mae-geri* ('front kick'). On the right, a Samurai gets his come-uppance (a rare event in medieval Japan). Oiko, apparently an ordinary pretty girl but in reality possessed of superhuman strength, is molested by the wrestler Saeki. To his astonished dismay she grabs him by the arm and drags him off to her cottage, where she forces him to eat rice balls that she has squeezed to the consistency of rock. It takes all the unfortunate wrestler's effort just to feed himself; but when finally released, he finds he has gained great strength and can easily defeat all his opponents. (Right, Oiko and Saeki, print by Yoshitoshi, Japan, 1889.)

Overleaf, The Samurai were perhaps the world's greatest warriors, and the sword was regarded as the warrior's soul. This print shows two actors in a Kabuki play based on events that took place during the wars of the 12th century. The figure on the right is using a thrusting action while the other parries it, reinforcing his action with a hand on the blunt edge of his sword. (Duel between Kameo Maru and Ario Maru, print by Kuniyoshi, Japan, c. 1845.)

A pair of temple guardians at the entrance to a Buddhist shrine. These fearsome figures, one yin (restraining inwardly) and the other yang (expressing outwardly), embody the protective powers that defend the doctrines of Buddhism from those who would corrupt them. Their sinewy musculature demonstrates mastery of breath-and-muscle control methods often used in martial arts systems. (China, 13th c.)

The strong spiritual emphasis in Japanese swordsmanship is expressed in stories of the supernatural origins of various combat systems.

In this print, Minamoto Yoshitsune (Ushikawa), a general in 12th-century Japan around whom a body of legend has grown, is shown receiving instruction in swordplay from the Tengu, mythical spirits related to the crow, who are holders of esoteric knowledge. Though of effeminate appearance, Yoshitsune acquired supernatural skill with the sword through the instruction of Sojobo, King of the local Tengu, who sits on the right.

Sojobo has in front of him scrolls containing the secret knowledge, and is holding a *vajra* (in Sanskrit), or *kongo*

(in Japanese). This is a ritual Buddhist object symbolizing the ignorance-destroying wisdom of enlightenment; its name can be translated as 'Diamond Sceptre' or 'Thunderbolt of Siva'. It is significant in that it bridges the gap between the spiritual and martial arts. At times Buddhist monks have used the *kongo*, or a small dumbbell-shaped stick of similar design, as a weapon which could transform a simple hand blow into a veritable thunderbolt.

(Ushikawa Encouraged in the Martial Arts at Kurama, triptych by Kunisada, Japan, c. 1815.)

The ancient Greeks practised many forms of combat, which are among the precursors of Western boxing and wrestling. Great power and skill were developed by these athletes, and stories are told of them which compare with the feats of modern Eastern martial artists. For instance, the boxer Milo of Crotona was capable of killing a bull with one blow from either hand; this incredible, if cruel, feat has been demonstrated by the modern Karate Master Oyama.

The vase painting shows a Greek boxer in combat with a centaur, using the 'one-two' (a left-right combination) familiar to modern boxers and usually ascribed to the famous Georges Carpentier. (Attic crater, Greece, 5th c. BC.)

Stick fighting between two exponents of Kalari Payat, a little-known art developed in Kerala in the South-west of India. Although India may have been the cradle of the spiritual martial arts, contemporary Indian systems are not widespread, and much knowledge has died out or is taught only secretly. In this picture, the great skill of the fighter on the right shows in his firmly balanced yet freely extended posture.

Many martial arts systems have been based on careful observation of animals fighting. Having no interfering rational mind, an animal moves freely and spontaneously in attack and defence, manifesting natural wisdom (the play of yin and yang in the T'ai Chi diagram; see p. 56). T'ai Chi itself was said to have originated when its founder, Chang San Feng, saw a crane fighting with a snake. The tiger, dragon, monkey, leopard and praying mantis have all been the inspiration of various styles. Compare the vortex-like movement of these two young stallions in the Camargue with the flow of water or the swirling action of an Aikido throw.

Some combat systems place great emphasis on leaping and high kicks. Demanding considerable skill, risky to use and often impractical in actual combat, these techniques are undeniably spectacular. Here two exponents of Kyokushinkai Karate (founded by Master Masutatsu Oyama) clash above a beach in Japan at sunset. Each is attempting a 'flying side kick' (*yoko tobi geri*) against the other.

Bamboo is an eternal symbol of the martial arts. It seems frail, yet in a storm even the toughest oak may be torn from its roots while the bamboo survives by yielding. Bamboo bends before a slight push, but springs back again when the push stops, returning the force back against the pusher. Firm and solid on the outside, yet empty within, not clinging to a fixed position yet maintaining a constancy of form through all external changes, the bamboo is a spiritual and martial arts teacher of the highest order. (Bamboo in Moonlight, ink painting on silk, artist unknown.)

Echoing the graceful, supple line of the bamboo, a master demonstrates a *kata* (prearranged formal exercise) using the *naginata* (a traditional halberd-like weapon with a curved blade).

A shrike perching on a dead branch, painted by Miyamoto Musashi. Musashi was perhaps the greatest Samurai ever. While still a youth, and a hot-tempered one at that, he developed amazing skill with the sword, and is said to have been defeated only once, by the founder of Jo-jitsu. His technique was direct and simple, free of traditional floweriness. If challenged, he was likely to strike down his challenger then and there, rather than to go through the ritual preparations.

He was also a master of painting (Fudo, 'The Way of the Brush'), which requires similar inner qualities to those necessary in the martial arts. Using black ink on soft paper, each stroke has to be perfect first time; the mastery shown in the long brush-stroke of the dead branch contains the spirit of Musashi's sword-stroke.

In later life he retired to a cave and wrote his famous book on strategy, *The Book of Five Rings*, which is one of the great classics on the martial arts. (Shrike on a Branch, ink drawing, Japan, 17th c.)

Eighty-two-year-old Master Noda of the Katori Shinto-Ryu, about to perform Iai-jitsu, the art of quick draw with the sword. Originally an essential and life-preserving skill, it embodies the essence of perfection in the martial arts in its simplicity, directness and power.

These two pictures – one of the face of Master Anzawa on the point of shooting his bow, the other of an *enso* (circle) painted by Torei, a pupil of Hakuin's – both show forth the indomitable integrity of the martial arts. The writing on the *enso* says: 'Every family can enjoy a fresh breeze and a bright moon; the spirit of Zen, too, is present everywhere.' (Brush drawing, Japan, 19th c.)

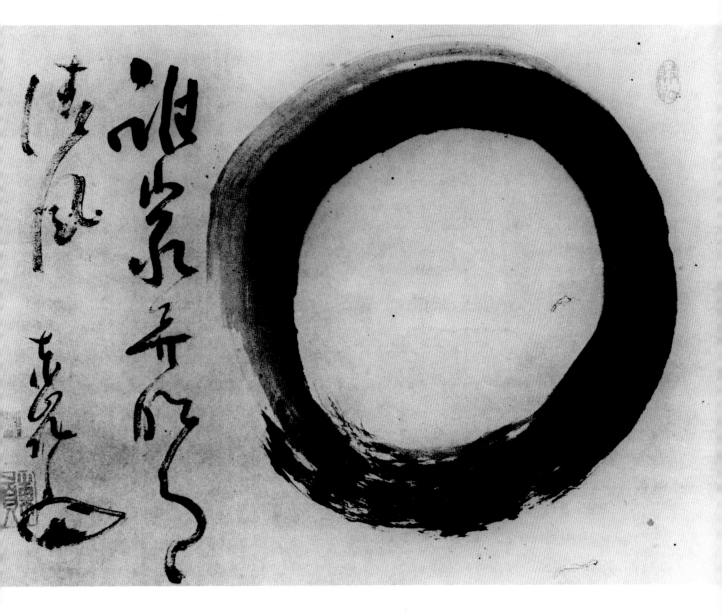

Although the influence of Zen in the martial arts is more in the public eye, Shinto, the native religion of Japan, also has a very large part to play. In his serene sitting, this Shinto priest manifests the tranquil, unified spirit which is like the ocean from which the surging waves of defence and attack can arise, and into which they again dissolve.

Themes

The vigour and freedom of the martial arts is conveyed in this fight between Master Shiokawa Terushige (armed with the Okinawan *sai*) and an opponent armed with a sword. This sort of formal yet spontaneous combat tests the skills of the participants to the utmost.

Grounding

As a tree draws nourishment from its roots, so a man draws power from the earth. Spirituality, strength and stability derive from 'grounding', implying both a firm contact with the earth and a good sense of one's physical body. Even in mechanical terms, strength ultimately comes from the earth; without solid ground under one's feet, the strongest muscle finds no purchase to act from – imagine Goliath standing on slippery ice and trying to push over a David whose feet are planted on firm soil.

Karate Master Kanazawa performing the first movement of the traditional Chinese health exercises, the Pa-tuan Chin, or 'Eight Brocades' (Hachi-Dankin in Japanese). This pose demonstrates a tree-like rooting as well as the flow of energy, like sap, right out to the fingertips.

圖形現兒嬰

他日雲飛方見真人朝上帝

潛龍今已化飛龍
變現神通不可窮
一朝跳出珠光外
內外無塵
神水洊波
滌灌根休
長養聖胎
渾身直到紫微宮

夫嬰兒之真
孕蘇呦之子
傳其術交葉
精兆其氣根
其神隨仙大
小俱得其真

此時丹熟更須慈母惜嬰兒

氣穴法名無盡藏
藏包於竅竅包空
我問空中誰氏子
他云是你主人翁

行住坐臥
抱護守雌
綿綿若存
念茲在茲

The central region in the body which corresponds to the earth is known as the *hara* in Japanese, *tan t'ien* in Chinese and *kath* in Arabic; in spiritual practices it is regarded as the centre of vitality and of the unification of mind and body. This drawing shows an early stage in the practice of Taoist Yoga: a breathing and visualization meditation which helps create the 'immortal foetus in the place of power', the seed for the development of a new and transformed self.

This sketch of a Sumo (Japanese wrestling) technique shows the use of vertical strength flowing up from the ground to sweep away an opponent; one is reminded of Hercules' victory over Antaeus by holding him off the earth, the source of his strength, and strangling him.

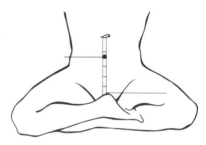

The location of the central point (*seika-no-itten*) of the *hara* is shown here; it is used as a focus for concentration in most of the martial arts. It is the point known in acupuncture as *ch'i hai* ('sea of energy') or 'Conception Vessel Six'.

The Western systems of Rolfing, Ideokinetics and the Alexander Technique emphasize the importance of the pelvic area in connecting the spine with the legs and thus providing stability and strength. This drawing details the muscular and bony configurations in the area. An inner, sensory awareness of these parts is extremely helpful in establishing physical and spiritual integration.

There are a great many techniques in the martial arts for improving grounding. Here the Japanese Taiki-Ken Master Kenichi Sawai demonstrates the basic exercise known as *neri* ('crawling'), which brings strength and resilience to the legs and hips as well as developing the sensitivity of the hands and fingers. *Neri* is done in slow motion, the feet moving in a zig-zag pattern.

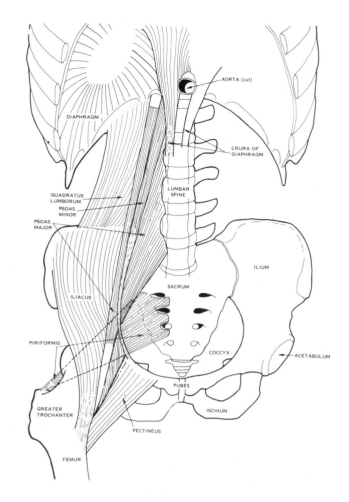

DIAPHRAGM
AORTA (cut)
CRURA OF DIAPHRAGM
LUMBAR SPINE
QUADRATUS LUMBORUM
PSOAS MINOR
PSOAS MAJOR
ILIUM
SACRUM
ILIACUS
PIRIFORMIS
COCCYX
ACETABULUM
PUBES
GREATER TROCHANTER
ISCHIUM
PECTINEUS
FEMUR

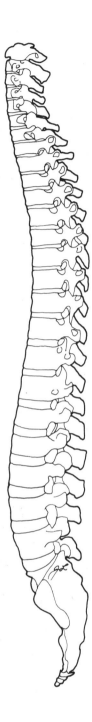

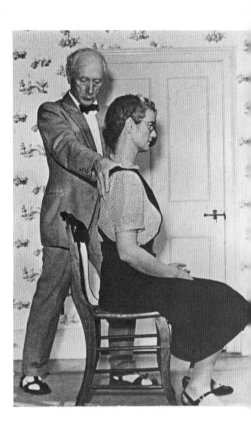

The Up

The source of energy, as explained in the preceding section, is the earth; but, without a direction to flow in, this energy remains inert. The basic direction of energy flow is *up*, an enlivening force of lightness in opposition to the downward drag of gravity. This flow is the movement of growth, of evolution towards higher states of consciousness. It is associated with choice and will; the direction is given by the head.

The gently curved, vertical spine, stretched elastically between heaven and earth, is indispensable for good health, both physical and spiritual. The image of the sky hook is an excellent aid to developing this condition. It is very important not to make any muscular effort to straighten the spine; simply imagine the sky hook and allow any change to happen without effort.

The Alexander Technique, here demonstrated by its founder, F.M. Alexander, teaches directly the correct 'use of the self'. In other words, it guides one towards the state of freedom and balance of body and mind that is the basis of effective performance in all activities.

The lightly poised head, drawn here by the Zen teacher and poet Paul Reps, is synonymous with clarity of mind and openness of spirit. The free neck is the key to the naturally vertical spine.

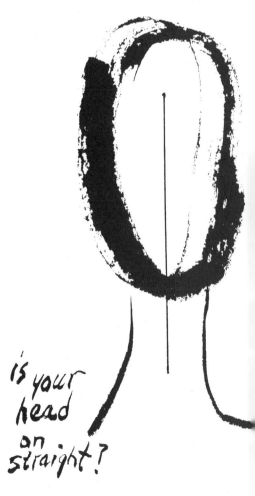

is your head on straight?

The free vertical spine is greatly emphasized in most martial arts. Here Master Kanei Uechi Jr, son of the founder of the Okinawan Karate system of Uechi-ryu, demonstrates perfect form in the performance of a *kata*, or prearranged formal exercise.

The practice of meditating under a waterfall, here performed by Master Gogen Yamaguchi ('The Cat') of the Goju-ryu Karate school, develops great intensity of upward energy flow as well as stabilizing body and mind.

In all animals the direction of movement is mediated by the head; and the spine, never cramped or shortened, lengthens along the line of motion.

Ki

The psychophysical energy known as *ki* is of fundamental importance in the martial arts. Developed by breathing and concentration and directed by the will, it can produce effects not only within the body but also at a distance from the practitioner.

Master Lew performs a breathing exercise from the Iron Palm system, designed to charge the hands with energy. Using this technique, a skilled practitioner can easily break a brick with a slap. A great master is capable of slapping the top of a stack of bricks and breaking only one, pre-selected brick in the pile!

Practitioners of Kalari Payat (a system native to Kerala, India) performing a ritual which precedes initiation into the art, in which the *ki* energy is channelled through the arms and hands out to the altar in the corner.

In the *kiai* (literally, 'energy union'), the energy of the entire body and spirit is focussed into a shout. Such a noise can of itself produce unconsciousness or even kill; it can also be used to revive someone from unconsciousness. It is frequently used in the martial arts to unify one's own powers and to create a momentary gap in the opponent's concentration. Here the swordsmaster Higuchi is caught at the instant of uttering the *kiai*.

A powerfully developed *ki* can be used in all parts of the body in many different ways. It can be used to forge the hand into a weapon of terrifying power, or it can be used to heal wounds and diseases. One of its most spectacular applications is as a protective shield; a master of *ki* can receive blows on any part of his body with impunity. It can even be used to give protection against edged weapons; in this photo of the famous Balinese trance dance, an initiate stabs a razor-sharp *kris* against his flesh without receiving the slightest scratch.

Ki has nothing to do with ordinary muscular strength. To the Western mind, the two photos of a contender for the title of Mr Universe and Woody Allen embody the extremes of physical strength and weakness. But the effortless power of *ki*, demonstrated in O-Sensei Uyeshiba's casual immoveability in the face of all efforts to unbalance him, has nothing to do with hard and bulky muscles.

Healing

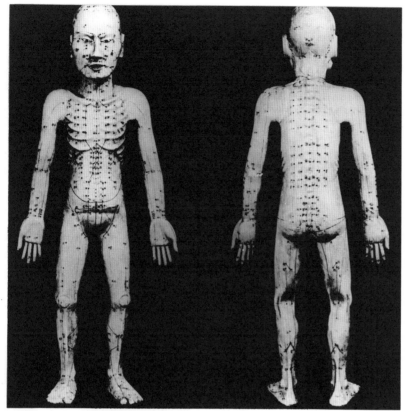

Most traditional martial arts schools teach healing techniques as well as the standard deadly fare. The basic principles behind both are identical: mastery of energy flow, clarity of mind, understanding of the body.

A bronze statue showing the acupuncture points and meridian lines. All disease is caused by deficiency or congestion of energy flow along these lines. (Copy of life-size bronze man originally cast in China, 1443.)

The use of a martial technique for healing. This method, from the Japanese Kuatsu system, uses a knee blow in the centre of the back (around the 6th dorsal vertebra) as a means of stimulating respiratory and cardiac function in an unconscious person. This technique is called *seoui-kuatsu*. (It goes without saying that an unskilled person should on no account attempt to use it.)

All martial arts systems have great health benefits. This traditional Taoist health exercise imitates the slow-motion drawing of a bow. Called *tso-you k'ai-kung ssu-she-tiao* ('Drawing a Bow to Left and Right as if Shooting an Eagle'), it is found in many ancient medical texts under the category of 'Life-prolonging Exercises', and has beneficial effects on the kidneys, lungs and circulation. Done with concentrated attention and coordinated with breathing from the belly, it develops the flow of *ki* energy in the same manner as do many martial arts exercises.

Just as a martial arts master may use his own *ki* flow to guide that of his opponent, so the conscious direction of *ki* can be used to heal by stimulating or calming the energy in another's body. Here a practitioner is encouraging a flow of healing energy through the man's leg.

A specific acupuncture point, no. 36 on the stomach meridian, four finger-widths from the base of the knee-cap, is good for strengthening the legs generally, as well as for calming nervous tension and improving the digestion. Martial arts practitioners are often taught methods of self-massage for improving energy flow and strength.

An early example of acupuncture anaesthesia. General Kwan Wun Cheong undergoing an operation on a wound from a poisoned arrow. As the surgeon (Wah Tor, 'The Divine Healer') scrapes the wound, the General is able to drink and joke with his friends, thanks to the pain-killing needles.

A hand formation from the Eagle Claw system, demonstrated by Master Douglas Wong. This is used principally for tearing at the throat.

Weapons

In the martial arts, most parts of the body can be used as lethal weapons. On the other hand, weapons themselves are treated as extensions of the body; to master the technique, the *ki* must be extended into and through the weapon itself. There are an incredible variety of different weapons, ranging from the simplest stick to the most elaborate Heath Robinson (Rube Goldberg) devices; it is therefore impossible to illustrate more than a very small selection.

Korean-born Master Masutatsu Oyama demonstrates three weapon formations of the hand: a calloused fist (*seiken*), spear-like fingertips (*nukite*) and the edge of the hand (*shuto*). Some schools emphasize long repetitions of toughening blows against a sand-bag or a bowl of peas for example, while others emphasize the development of internal

energy (*ki*) and the extension of this energy through the striking weapon.

In the effective use of weapons formed from the human body, a knowledge of the body's vulnerable, or vital, points is important. These points correspond to the acupuncture points used in healing. Each martial arts school has its chart of deadly areas; these charts in the past would have been very closely guarded. In China, this knowledge was developed to such a pitch that a master could, with a light touch, produce any desired effect on his unfortunate victim, ranging from partial paralysis, through various disease conditions, to the famous delayed 'death touch' which would cause death after a predetermined lapse of time. This chart shows the secret vital points from the traditional Japanese school of Muso-ryu. (It must be pointed out that for those who have not been shown the exact location of these points, this chart carries no useful information – it was drawn to serve as a mnemonic rather than as a teaching device.)

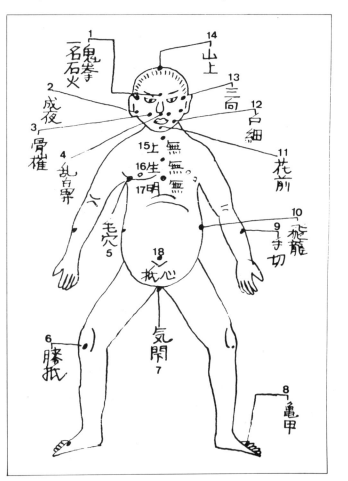

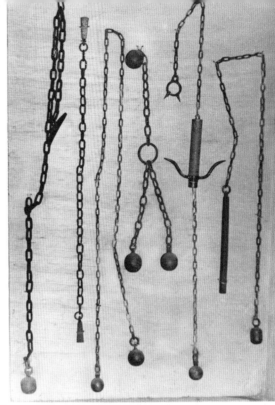

The stick is a universal weapon, and in the opinion of many, the *jo* (oak staff) is the most effective of all. Here O-Sensei Uyeshiba demonstrates the countering of a *jo* attack using a wooden sword, or *bokken*. As Tamura-sensei attacks with a thrust of the *jo*, O-Sensei angles his body lightly forward and to the right, avoiding the thrust and simultaneously counterattacking with his *bokken*. This sliding movement demonstrates a basic principle of Aikido, a fundamental body skill which applies equally to weapon and empty-hand techniques.

Two women practitioners of Kalari Payat practising attack and defence with short sticks. A weapon in its own right, the stick can also be used as a substitute for edged weapons, which are more dangerous for a beginner to practise with.

On Okinawa, during the period of Japanese control which started about 400 years ago, the villagers were forbidden to carry weapons (including the *sai*, a three-pronged fork very effective in countering a sword attack). To maintain their capacity to defend themselves against the oppression of the occupying forces, they developed Karate to a particularly high degree, achieving the capacity to punch through armour with a bare fist and to deflect and dodge sword attacks. They also developed common agricultural implements into deadly weapons; illustrated above left are the *jo* (top), two *nunchaku*, derived from a threshing flail (centre), two *tonfa*, implements used for husking rice (left) and two *sai* (right). These have since become divorced from their original use and are established as weapons in their own right. Also illustrated are the easily concealed throwing stars and spikes (*shuriken*).

Above, An assortment of Japanese chain weapons, still used by a few schools today. Swung in an arc, these can entangle an opponent's sword or trap his feet like a bolas; the weighted free end could deliver an armour-crushing blow.

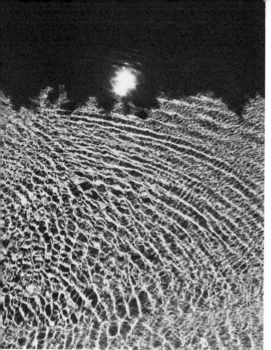

Spontaneity

The profoundly disciplined martial arts master responds to attack without conscious thought or deliberation. But his reaction is no thoughtless reflex or formless jerk; it is a precise and fully appropriate action in accord with the principles of natural movement.

The ripples in water emerge without artifice or plan, yet they are perfect and harmonious manifestations of the laws of wave and flow. The Zen garden, with its rock mountains and sand waves, embodies the harmony and controlled spontaneity which characterizes the masterly performance of the martial arts. Having 'returned to the pre-birth body', uncovering through long discipline the natural energy and movement of the unified body/mind, the master's action is as perfect and spontaneous as that of the wind and waves. (Zen garden, Ryoanji Temple, Kyoto, Japan.)

In this picture sequence a Karate master splits an arrow fired at him from point-blank range. Such a feat, which is used as a training exercise in several martial arts schools, clearly demands a controlled spontaneity of the highest order.

In this Karate sparring exercise, developed by Master Egami, the opponents stand at some distance from each other. On the teacher's signal, they both attack; but the point of the exercise is that their actions should be simultaneous with the command of the teacher (not merely very shortly after it). This requires a spontaneity of action that transcends speed of reflex and approaches the telepathic. The participants do not react in response to some internal thought or external stimulus; their openness of mind allows a synchronistic harmony with their environment and thus a truly appropriate spontaneous action.

Hokusai's woodcut of a warrior on horseback plunging down a precipice to escape his pursuers captures the paradoxical nature of spontaneity – the complete passive abandon of the rider (the thinking, planning mind) and the furious and precise rush of the horse (the whole intuitive body). (Woodcuts from the Manga, by Hokusai, Japan, 18th–19th c.)

No mind

The fundamental state of meditative practice is also the prerequisite for mastery in the martial arts. The mind is completely open and free, and takes in everything without distortion or grasping. There is no thought of self or other, no emotion of fear or desire. Mind and body, inner and outer, are in a harmony so complete that it embraces struggle and death.

This painting of a sage in meditation shows the tranquillity and freedom that are the essence of the martial arts. (Ink drawing on paper by Kang-Hui-An, Korea, 15th c.)

This landscape conveys the open, spacious state of No Mind, implying through the mists which obscure the mountains the all-encompassing space which permeates all things. (Travellers in a Landscape, ink and colours on silk, Hiroshige school, China 19th c.)

Karate Master Egami in a *kamae* or combat-ready stance. His awareness shines out so completely that his opponent can find no gap to enter.

Above right, Aikido Master Saito-sensei prepares for *kokyu-ho* ('Breath Throw'). No thought of opposition enters his mind, which is calm and undisturbed. But in the next instant, his opponents will find themselves flying through the air with no awareness of how they got there. If he were to struggle or to fix his mind on the idea of being gripped, he would be unable to shift their combined strength.

The spirit of No Mind manifested at the highest levels of Aikido. O-Sensei Uyeshiba (below) throws his opponent effortlessly, without even touching him. Offering no resistance, mental or physical, he allows the attacker's momentum to carry him on to his own downfall.

Further reading

Alexander, F. Matthias, *The Alexander Technique: The Essential Writings of F. Matthias Alexander* (ed. E. Maisel), London 1974; published in USA as *The Resurrection of the Body*, New York 1974.

Barlow, Wilfred, *The Alexander Principle: How to Use Your Body*, London 1973; published in USA as *The Alexander Technique*, New York 1974.

Brown, Olive, *Your Innate Power*, London and Winchester (Mass.) 1967.

Bubba Free John, *Conscious Exercise and the Transcendental Sun*, Clearlake Highlands 1977.

Cheng Man-Ch'ing, and Robert W. Smith, *T'ai Chi: The Supreme Ultimate Exercise for Health, Sport and Self-defense*, Rutland and Tokyo 1966.

Chung-Yuan, Chang, *Creativity and Taoism*, New York 1970, London 1975

DeLong Miller, Roberta, *Psychic Massage*, London and New York 1975.

DeMile, James W. *Tao of Wing Chun Do* (vols. 1, 2), Santa Rosa 1977, 1978.

Draeger, Don, and Robert W. Smith, *Asian Fighting Arts*, New York 1969.

Dürckheim, Karlfried von, *Hara: The Vital Centre of Man* (trs. from the German by S.-M. van Kospoth and E. R. Healey), London and Winchester (Mass.) 1977

Huang, Al Chung-Liang, *Embrace Tiger, Return to Mountain: The Essence of T'ai Chi*, Moab 1973, London 1978.

Huard, Pierre, and Ming Wong, *Oriental Methods of Mental and Physical Fitness* (trs. D. M. Smith), New York 1977.

Lee, Bruce, *Tao of Jeet Kune Do*, Burbank 1975.

Leggett, Trevor, *Zen and The Ways*, Boulder 1977, London 1978.

Leonard, George, *The Ultimate Athlete*, New York 1975.

Mattson, George E., *The Way of Karate*, Rutland and Tokyo 1963.

Minick, Michael, *The Kung-Fu Exercise Book: Health Secrets of Ancient China*, London and Cedar Knolls 1977.

Musashi, Miyamoto, *A Book of Five Rings* (trs. from the Japanese by V. Harris), London 1973, New York 1974.

Reps, Paul, *Juicing*, New York 1978.

Rolf, Ida, *Rolfing*, Santa Monica 1977.

Saito, Morihiro, *Traditional Aikido*, vols 1–5, New York 1973–76.

Smith, Robert W., *Chinese Boxing: Masters and Methods*, New York 1974.

——, *Pa Kua: Chinese Boxing for Fitness and Self-defense*, New York 1967.

Suzuki, Daisetz Teitaro, *Zen and Japanese Culture*, London and Princeton 1959.

Tarthang Tulku, *Gesture of Balance: A Guide to Awareness*, Emeryville 1976.

——, *Time, Space and Knowledge: A New Vision*, Emeryville 1977.

Todd, Mabel E., *The Thinking Body: A Study of the Balancing Forces of Dynamic Man*, New York 1975.

Westbrook, Adele, and Oscar Ratti, *Aikido and the Dynamic Sphere*, New York 1970.

Wilhelm, R., and C. G. Jung, *The Secret of the Golden Flower: A Chinese Book of Life* (trs. from the German by C. F. Baynes), London 1962, New York 1970.

Acknowledgments

The objects shown in the plates and themes sections (pp. 48–95) are in the collections of:

Florence, Museo Archeologico 70; London, British Museum 74, 93 below, 94 below; Victoria and Albert Museum 52, 53, 54, 61, 63, 64–5, 68–9; Nanking, Natural History Museum 88 above; Seoul, National Museum of Korea 94 above; Washington D.C., Freer Gallery of Art 66, 67.

Photographs were supplied by courtesy of:

Aspen Academy of the Martial Arts 57; K. Chiba 50; Bruce Colman 85 below; Doubleday & Co. 84 below (from P. Reps, *Juicing*); John Dugger 60; Michael Finn 59, 75, 91 above r.; Harper & Row Publications Inc. 89 above (from R. DeLong Miller, *Psychic Massage*); Michael Holford 64–5; Honbu Dojo 51; *Inside Kung Fu* 86 r., 90 below l.; Japan Publications Inc. 73, 90 3rd from top, 92 centre and below (from M. Oyama, *This is Karate*), 91 centre, 95 below (from M. Saito, *Traditional Aikido*, vol. 1), 83 below (from K. Sawai, *The Essence of Kung Fu: Taiki-ken*); Keystone Press Agency 62, 71, 80, 86 above, 87 above l. and below l., 91 below; M. Kanetsuka 82 centre; Kodansha International Ltd 90 above, 93 above, 95 above l. (from S. Egami, *The Way of Karate: Beyond Technique*); William MacQuitty 52, 66, 67, 82 above, 87 above r., 92 above r.; Mansell Collection 70; André Nocquet 87 below r.; Peabody Publishing Co. 85 above l. (from G. E. Mattson, *Uechiryu Karate Do*); Denis Postle 92 above l.; Michel Random 49, 77, 78, 81, 85 r., 86 below; Sakamoto Photo Research Laboratory 76; H. Silvester-Rapho 72; Eileen Tweedy 53, 54, 61, 63, 68–9; Zefa 56.

Picture research by Marian Berman

Illustrations in the main text drawn by Georgie Glen and Elizabeth Wickham